Anonymous

Acts of the General Assembly of the State of Florida

Anonymous

Acts of the General Assembly of the State of Florida

ISBN/EAN: 9783744762298

Printed in Europe, USA, Canada, Australia, Japan

Cover: Foto ©Suzi / pixelio.de

More available books at **www.hansebooks.com**

THE

ACTS AND RESOLUTIONS

ADOPTED BY THE

General Assembly of Florida,

AT AN

ADJOURNED SESSION,

BEGUN AND HELD AT THE CAPITOL, IN THE CITY OF TALLAHAS-
SEE, ON MONDAY, NOVEMBER 28, 1859.

PUBLISHED BY AUTHORITY OF LAW,

UNDER THE DIRECTION OF THE ATTORNEY GENERAL.

Tallahassee:

'OFFICE OF THE FLORIDIAN AND JOURNAL,

PRINTED BY DYKE & CARLISLE,

1859.

TITLES

OF

ACTS AND RESOLUTIONS,

Passed at an Adjourned Session of the General Assembly,

1859.

CHAPTER 996. An act to amend the Militia and Patrol Laws of this State.

997. An act concerning Sheriffs and Coroners.

998. An act to amend the Attachment Laws of this State.

999. An act to amend the Laws now in force in this State relative to Ejectment Suits.

1,000. An act to provide for the payment of Constables' fees for summoning Juries of Inquest and attendance on the same.

1,001. An act concerning Costs and Fees.

1,002. An act to extend the time for collecting Taxes in this State.

1,003. An act to grant retail Licenses in the State of Florida.

1,004. An act to amend an act entitled an act to amend an act to establish the Ad Valorem System of Taxation, approved January 15th, 1859.

1,005. An act for the protection and disposal of Wrecked and Derelict Goods in the State of Florida.

1,006. An act to require Physicians and Surgeons to file certified copies of their Diplomas.

1,007. An act to prevent the unnecessary use of Fire-arms in the State of Florida on Sunday.

1,008. An act to allow Spiritous Liquors to be drank where sold.

1,009. An act to amend the law allowing appeals from the decisions of the Boards of County Commissioners in this State.

1,010. An act for the payment of the Florida Volunteers called into service under the requisition of the Governor of this State for services rendered previous to their being mustered in, during the years 1855–'6.

1,011. An act to amend an act entitled an act to establish Common Schools and repeal certain acts in relation thereto, approved January 1st, 1853.

1,012. An act to allow Additional Compensation to County Commissioners.

1,013. An act in relation to Courts of Probate in this State.

1,014. An act in relation to Records.

1,015. An act to repeal in part the 24th section of the act entitled an act to provide for and encourage a liberal system of Internal Improvements in this State, approved Jan. 6, 1855.

1,016. An act concerning Roads.

1,017. An act in relation to the Boundary Line between this State and Georgia.

1,018. An act to provide for the payment of costs by Plaintiffs in the Western Judicial Circuit.

1,019. An act to authorize the Board of Education of State Seminary West of the Suwannee to confer Collegiate Degrees.

1,020. An act to authorize the Trustees of the Internal Improvement Fund to drain out the channel of the Oclawaha River in this State, for the purpose of improving the navigation of the same, and for other purposes.

1,021. An act in relation to the Gulf City and Interior Railroad Company and the Pensacola and Georgia Railroad Company.

1,022. An act to incorporate the Apalachicola and New Orleans Steam Navigation Company.

1,023. An act to incorporate the Apalachicola and Columbus steamboat Company.

1,024. An act declaring the Perdido River Navigable.

1,025. An act to incorporate the Lake City and Suwannee Railroad Company.

1,026. An act more fully defining the duties of Tax Assessors and Collectors for the City of Pensacola.

1,027. An act to amend an act entitled an act to amend an act entitled an act to incorporate the Town of Quincy, approved February 12, 1857, approved January 13, 1859.

1,028. An act to correct an error in the printed act entitled an act to incorporate the City of Lake City.

1,029. An act to amend an act amending the Charter of the City of Pensacola, for the purpose of extending the powers of the City to aid in the construction of the Alabama and Florida Railroad in Florida, approved December 21st, 1858.

1,030. An act to amend an act entitled an act to incorporate the City of Atseena Otie.

1,031. An act to authorize the Mayor and Aldermen of the City of Pensacola to elect a Public Weigher of Cotton.

1,032. An act to secure the right of way to the St. Johns and Indian River Canal, and for other purposes.

1,033. An act to grant alternate sections of Swamp and Overflowed Lands to the Perdido Railroad Company.

1,034. An act to change the time of holding the Circuit Court in the counties of Hamilton and Taylor in the Middle Judicial Circuit of Florida.

1,035. An act to amend an act to provide for the recording of Marks and Brands of Cattle shipped from the counties of Manatee and Hillsborough, passed at the 9th General Assembly, approved by the Governor January 13, 1859.

1,036. An act to amend an act entitled an act organizing the county of Volusia, approved Jan. 29th, 1854.

1,037. An act for filling Offices in the County of Brevard.

1,038. An act to make the Road Laws of Duval County, now in force applicable to Manatee.

1,039. An act to amend an act entitled an act to divide the County of Duval, and organize a new county to be called Clay County, approved by the Governor December 31st, 1858.

1,040. An act in reference to Common Schools in the county of Walton.

1,041. An act relative to the Office of Circuit Court Clerk in the County of Washington.

1,042. An act authorizing a Bridge Tax in Walton County.

1,043. An act to create and regulate Pilotage at the Port of Bay Port, in the county of Hernando.

1,044. An act amending the Pilot Laws for the Bay and Harbor of the City of Pensacola, of the State of Florida.

1,045. An act repealing certain acts passed in relation to the County Officers of Calhoun County.

1,046. An act to alter and define the line between Gadsden and Liberty Counties.

1,047. An act to correct an error in a printed bill entitled an act to create the Counties of Suwannee and New River.

1,048. An act to change the Boundary Line between Columbia and Suwannee Counties.

1,049. An act to regulate the fees of Notary Publics in the County of St Johns.

1,050. An act to unite the offices of Judge of Probate and Clerk of Circuit Court in Volusia County.

1,051. An act for the benefit of the heirs of the estate of James E. Hendry, deceased.

1,052. An act for the relief of Noah P. Suggs of Lafayette County.

1,053. An act for the relief of John M. Hill.

1,054. An act for the relief of John Addison and others.

1,055. An act for the relief of Simeon A. Edwards.

1,056. An act to correct an error in an act approved January 15th, 1859, entitled an act for the relief of Josiah Gates and other persons therein named, citizens of Manatee county.

1,057. An act for the relief of Samuel B. Williford the County Surveyor of Jackson county.

1,058. An act for the relief of H. T. Blocker.

1,059. An act for the relief of Allen Gibson of Marion county and Solomon Haliday of Alachua county.

1,060. An act for the relief of Mathias F. Papy.

1,061. An act for the relief of Andrew J. Moore and William S. Dilworth.

1,062. An act for the relief of Isaac N. Shepard, Guardian of the minor heirs of Henry N. Shepard, late of Gadsden county, deceased.

1,063. An act for the relief of Isaac N. Shepard of Gadsden County.

1,064. An act for the relief of Susan Pearce, administratrix, and James T. Lester, administrator, of the estate of William Pearce.

1,065. An act for the relief of Harrison Fairbank.

1,066. An act to establish a Ferry across the Oclawaha River.

1,067. An act to authorize Spencer Price of Levy County to establish a Ferry from No. 4 on the main land to the western terminus of the Florida Railroad on Way Key, thence across the bay to the city of Atseena–Otie.

1,068. An act to authorize George W. Martin to establish a Ferry across the Suwannee River at Fayetteville.

1,069. An act to allow William W. Tucker, of Jefferson County, to assume the management of his own estate.

1,070. An act to authorize Joseph D. Smith to assume the management of his own estate.

1,071. An act to authorize Edmond N. Everitt, of Washington county, to assume the management of his own property.

1,072. An act to authorize William F. Green, of Gadsden county, to contract and be contracted with.

1,073. An act to empower John W. Broxson and Isaac Broxson to assume the management of their own estates.

1,074. An act to empower Littleberry Manning to assume the management of his own estate.

1,075. An act to empower Charles Maltby West, a minor, of Leon county, to assume the management of his own estate.

1,076. An act to authorize John S. Addison, a minor, of Marion county, to assume the management of his own estate.

1,077. An act to empower David Franklin Houck to assume the management of his own estate.

1,078. An act to authorize Minor W. Walker, of Jefferson county, to assume the management of his own estate.

1,079. An act to empower Susan M. Croom, a minor, of Leon county, to assume the management of her own estate.

1,080. An act to empower Thomas J. Chace, a minor, of Jefferson county, to assume the management of his own estate.

1,081. An act to authorize David Newnan Cone, a minor, of Columbia county, to assume the management of his own estate.

1,082. An act to change the name of George Frisbee.

1,083. An act to change the name of George Gibbs Smith.

1,084. An act to change the name of Hugh Martin Newsoms to Hugh Martin Keen.

1,085. An act to change the name of Mary King to Mary Hancock.

1,086. An act to change the name of Andrew J. Revells of Madison County, to that of Andrew J. Duncan.

1,087. An act for the relief of Alexander Douglas, Peter C. Wilkins and Kenneth McCaskill.

1,088. An act making appropriations for the expenses of the State Government for the fiscal years of 1859 and 1860.

RESOLUTIONS.

1. Resolution relative to the Common School Laws.

2. Resolution relative to the establishment of the Boundary line between the State of Georgia and the State of Florida.

3. Resolution with regard to certain persons who have circulated or aided in circulating an Incendiary publication entitled "the Impending Crisis of the South."

4. Resolution to empower the Governor of the State to sell certain bonds.

5. Resolution for the relief of the Comptroller of the State.

6. Resolution relative to the office of Register of U. S. Lands at Tallahassee.

7. Resolution to change Mail Route No. 6543.

8. Resolution urging upon Congress to establish a fort and other necessary fortifications.

9. Joint resolution allowing the claims of Captain Thomas Hughey.

10. Resolution for the relief of Donald Cameron.

11. Resolution authorizing the Treasurer to pay Fifty Dollars for writing up the Journals of the Senate.

12. Resolution for the relief of certain parties holding State Witness and Jury scrip.

13. Joint resolution for the relief of Andrew J. Lanier of Lafayette County.

14. Resolution for the relief of J. C. Crosby, late Sheriff of Escambia County.

15. Resolution for the relief of William Newborn, a soldier of the war of 1812 and 1814.

LAWS

OF THE

STATE OF FLORIDA,

Passed at an Adjourned Session of the General Assembly,

1859.

M. S. PERRY, Governor. F. L. VILLEPIGUE, Secretary of State. T. W. BREVARD, Comptroller of Public Accounts. CHARLES H. AUSTIN, State Treasurer. M. D. PAPY, Attorney General. JOHN FINLAYSON, President of the Senate. J. E. BOWDEN, Secretary of the Senate. JOHN B. GALARAITH, Speaker of the House. M. F. PAPY, Clerk of the House.

1859.

———◆———

CHAPTER 996.—[No. 1.]

AN ACT to amend the Militia and Patrol Laws of this State.

SECTION 1. *Be it enacted by the Senate and House of Representatives of the State of Florida in General Assembly convened,* That the Commission of each and every officer of Militia of this State, of every rank, both field, staff and line, be, and they are hereby vacated.

SEC 2. *Be it further enacted,* That the Militia shall be divided into two divisions and five Brigades. The Militia west of the Suwannee river shall compose the first Division, and the Militia east of the said river shall compose the second Division ; each Judicial Circuit shall compose a Brigade, and each Senatorial District shall compose a Regiment, and each Regiment shall be divided into two Bat-

Commissions prior to this act to be vacated.

Militia divided into divisions, brigades, regiments and battalions, &c.

2

talions, and each Regiment shall take the number of its
Senatorial District.

SEC. 3. *Be it further enacted,* That it shall be the duty
Governor to of the Governor to order an election to be held throughout
order an election
to fill all Militia the State on the first Monday of May next, for the election
offices. of Division, Brigade, Regimental and Company officers, of
the Militia of the State. Thirty day's notice of such election shall be given in all the newspapers of the State.

SEC. 4. *Be it further enacted,* That it shall be the duty
County Com- of the Board of County Commissioners, in each and every
missioners to di-
vide their coun- County of this State, to divide the County into Beats, and
ty into Beats to describe particularly on the records of their respective
within 90 days
from the passage Boards, immediately, the boundary lines of each beat so
of this act. laid off by the aforesaid Boards, as well as all alterations
that they may hereafter make, and post a copy of the same
at the doors of their respective Court Houses within five
days after each Beat shall have been so made; and each
Beat shall contain not less than forty-five, nor more than
one hundred men, subject to Military duty; and upon failure
of any Board of Commissioners to perform said duty within ninety days from the passage of this act, each and every
Commissioner of the Board of County Commissioners who
shall fail to divide their respective Counties into Beats as
required by this act, shall be fined in the sum of fifty dollars, to be recovered in any Court of competent jurisdiction
in this State, or by indictment before the Circuit Court of
the County.

SEC. 5. *Be it further enacted,* That it shall be the duty
County Com- of the respective Board of County Commissioners to desig-
missioners to de-
signate a place nate a place in each Beat in their respective Counties, at
to hold Militia which place so designated all elections for Military officers
elections. shall hereafter be held.

SEC. 6. *Be it further enacted,* That it shall be the duty
Judge of Pro- of the Judge of Probate of each County to appoint three
bate to appoint
Inspectors. suitable persons in each Beat as inspectors of said election
ordered by the Governor by this act, and the Judge of Probate shall give notice of the time and place and the names
of the inspectors of each Beat to hold said election, and
Election, how shall publish the same by posting notice thereof, ten days
held. prior to the election, at the place in each Beat where said
election shall be held, and said election shall be held as is
now provided by law for Militia officers, and the said inspectors of each Beat shall make return of said election to

the Judge of Probate of the County within three days after
such election.

SEC. 7. *Be it further enacted*, That it shall be the duty of the Judge of Probate of each County to summon two suitable persons, which persons, together with the Judge of Probate, shall form the board of canvassers, of the County for Militia elections, and said board of canvassers shall canvass the returns of the several Beats on the third day after the election ; and said board of canvassers shall make return to the Secretary of State of the result of said election, certifying the name of each person voted for, the office which he was voted for, and the number of votes by him received ; and said board of canvassers shall certify to the same under the seal of the Probate Court, and shall notify the Secretary of State by annexing to their certificate of election a statement of any failure to fill any Militia office, and to recommend suitable persons to be appointed to fill the office for which there has been a failure to elect in their County or in any Beat, and shall send said certificate to the Secretary of State by mail immediately after the said returns are canvassed.

County canvassers of election returns, their duty.

Where failure to elect occurs, Board of Commissioners to recommend persons to the Governor to be appointed.

SEC. 8. *Be it further enacted*, That the Secretary of State, Treasurer and Comptroller shall, thirty days after the holding of the said election, canvass the returns made to the Secretary of State, and publish the result of said election in some newspaper published at the Capital, and shall certify the result to the Governor.

State canvassers, their duty.

SEC. 9. *Be it further enacted*, That it shall be the duty of the Governor to appoint and commission a suitable person to fill any Militia office for which there had been a failure to elect, and the officer or officers so appointed shall be obliged to serve one year or until others are elected to fill their places, under the same penalties as though they had been duly elected: *Provided, however*, That no officer thus appointed shall be required to appear in uniform.

Governor to appoint to fill all failures to elect officers.

Persons appointed obliged to serve.

SEC. 10. *Be it further enacted*, That it shall be the duty of each Captain to make out a correct Muster Roll of all persons subject to militia duty in his Beat, and to forward to the Colonel of his Regiment said Muster Roll within thirty days after he shall have qualified under his commission, under a penalty of Fifty Dollars.

Captain to make out Muster Rolls within 30 days.

SEC. 11. *Be it further enacted*, That it shall be the duty of each Colonel to forward a correct Muster Roll of his Regi-

Colonel to forward Muster Roll of Regim'nt within 60 days.

ment to the Adjutant General of the State within sixty days after he has qualified as Colonel, under a penalty of Two Hundred Dollars: *Provided. however*, That all Muster Rolls after the first return required in this act shall thereafter be made according to military rules.

Persons sub- ject to Militia duty, how ex- empted from service.

SEC. 12. *Be it further enacted*, That any private shall be exempt from Militia duty upon his paying into the hands of the Sheriff of the county, taking his receipt for the same, the sum of six dollars per annum, together with twenty per cent. on his State Tax, and the person so exempted shall present said receipt to the Captain of his Beat, and it shall be the duty of the Sheriff to keep a list of the persons who have paid the said sums for the purpose of being exempted from Militia duty and to forward a copy of said list, together with the amount of money by him collected, and pay the same over to the Paymaster General of the State quarterly, under a penalty of one hundred dollars, together with the sum by him unlawfully detained, which shall be recovered by rule before the Circuit Court against said Sheriff, and said sum recovered on the judgment rendered on the rule shall be paid over to the Paymaster General of the State, and said rule shall be brought by the Solicitor of the Circuit in the name of the Governor.

Sheriff to keep list of exempti'ns and pay to Pay- master General.

Rule against Sheriff for fail're to pay over to Paymaster Gen'l

Captains to for- ward list of per- sons exempted from militia duty to Adj't General.

SEC. 13. *Be it further enacted*, That it shall be the duty of the Captain of each Beat to forward quarterly to the Ad- jutant General of the State a correct list of the persons ex- empted from Militia duty, and the amount by them paid to the Sheriff and the date of the payment, under penalty of fifty dollars.

Military fund.

SEC. 14. *Be it further enacted*, That the sums received by the Paymaster General for exemption from Militia duty shall constitute a Military Fund for the purpose of purchas- ing arms and accoutrements for the Volunteer Companies and for other Military purposes: *Provided, however*, That said Volunteer Companies shall be completely uniformed, and shall drill at least once in two months, and the Captain of each Volunteer Company, desirous of obtaining the aid of this fund, shall certify to the Adjutant General the number of men in his Company, their uniform which they at the time wear, and the full particulars of the state and condition of his Company, and the number of times they hold com- pany drill.

Volunteer'com- panies desirous of obtaining aid from military fund, require- ments.

SEC. 15. *Be it further enacted*, That said Military Fund

shall be placed at the disposal and subject to the order of the Governor for the purpose of purchasing arms and accoutrements and for Military purposes as aforesaid.

Military fund subject to the order of Governor for certain purposes.

SEC. 16. *Be it further enacted*, That each and every officer of militia, who shall be elected and qualified under his commission, shall he compelled to serve for the term of two years, unless he is promoted or removes from the military district for which he was elected, under the following penalties: A General of Division or Brigade, one thousand dollars; a Field Officer, five hundred dollars, and a Company Officer, three hundred dollars, to be recovered by indictment before the Circuit Court, to be paid to the Paymaster General for the Military Fund.

Officers who have qualified compelled to serve for two years.

SEC. 17. *Be it further enacted*, That each and every commissioned officer of militia who shall fail to perform any military duty required of him by his superior officer, or by the law of this State, not specifically prescribed, shall be indicted in the Circuit Court, and fined not less than fifty nor more than one hundred dollars, at the discretion of the Court.

Penalty for non-performance of duty by officers.

SEC. 18. *Be it further enacted*, That each and every commissioned officer of Volunteer and Militia, after the expiration of six months from the date of his commission, shall appear in full uniform on all military service, and shall be entitled to appear in uniform whenever he may choose to do so; and any person or persons who shall not appear in full uniform, as required, or shall wear uniform to which he is not entitled by law, shall be fined not less than Fifty Dollars nor more than One Hundred Dollars, at the discretion of the Court.

Officers compelled to uniform.

SEC. 19. *Be it further enacted*, That the Company, Battalion, Regimental, Brigade and Division musters shall be held and formed as now by law directed.

Musters, how held.

SEC. 20. *Be it further enacted*, That all Returns now by law required for Militia shall be evidence of the facts therein stated, in any Court in this State: *Provided, however*, That such Return shall be sworn to by the officer making the same.

Militia returns made evidence.

SEC. 21. *Be it further enacted*, That all penalties and fines imposed by this act, and the act to which this is an amendment, under fifty dollars, shall be recovered by action of debt before any Justice of the Peace, and all sums over fifty dollars, by indictment before the Circuit Court,

Penalties and fines, how recovered.

which sums shall be paid to the Paymaster General for the Military Fund.

Solicitors to receive $10 for each conviction.

SEC. 22. *Be it further enacted*, That the Solicitor of the Circuit where such indictment is found for a violation of this act, or the act to which this is an amendment, shall be entitled to a fee of ten dollars for each conviction, to be taxed in the bill of costs against the defendant.

Paymaster Gen'l to give bond.

SEC. 23. *Be it further enacted*, That the Paymaster General shall give bond, to be approved by the Governor, in the sum of ten thousand dollars, conditioned for the faithful performance of his duties, and shall be entitled to a commission of five per cent. on all moneys received by him, and shall make report to the Governor whenever called on by him to do so.

Fines by Court Martials abolis'd

Judge of Circuit Court to charge Grand Jury.

SEC. 24. *Be it further enacted*, That fines by Courts Martial are hereby abolished, and it shall be the duty of the Circuit Court Judges to give this act and the act to which this is an amendment specially in charge to the Grand Juries of their circuit at each term of the Court.

Duty of Solicitor.

SEC. 25. *Be it further enacted*, That the different Solicitors of the Circuits of this State be and they are hereby required to bring each and every offender of this act, and the act to which this is an amendment, before the Court by indictment, to be punished for violation thereof.

Captain to attend and inform Solicitor of all violations of militia law.

SEC. 26. *Be it further enacted*, That it shall be the duty of each Captain to attend the Solicitor of the Circuit and inform said Solicitor of all the violations of the Militia Law in his county, or which shall come to his knowledge, whether committed by a commissioned officer or any other person, and of which the Circuit Court has jurisdiction, and on failure so to do, each Captain so offending shall be liable to be

Captain to institute suits in Justice's Court for violations of militia duty.

fined not less than Fifty Dollars nor more than Five Hundred Dollars, at the discretion of the Court; and each Captain of each Volunteer and Militia Company shall institute suits in any Justice's Court to recover any fine or penalty imposed by law for militia offences and which is made within the Justice's jurisdiction by this act, and said suits shall be

All executions from Justice's Court to be placed in the hands of the Sheriff.

brought in the name of the State of Florida, and the execution shall be placed in the hands of the Sheriff, to be by him collected and paid over as is by this act required, and for failure so to do, each Captain so failing to institute suit as required by this act, shall be fined not less than Fifty nor more than One Thousand dollars, at the discretion of the Court.

SEC. 27. *Be it further enacted*, That the Governor shall cause this act, together with all the Militia Laws not repealed by this act, to be arranged and published in pamphlet form and distributed to the Judge of Probate of each county, and also furnish each commissioned officer with a copy thereof. *Governor to have the militia acts arranged and published.*

SEC. 28. *Be it further enacted*, That the Volunteer Companies shall be governed by this act and the act to which this is an amendment. *Volunteer companies govern'd by militia laws.*

SEC. 29. *Be it further enacted*, That all laws and parts of laws inconsistent with this act be and they are hereby repealed. *Repeal of acts inconsistent with this act.*

Passed the House December 21, 1859. Passed the Senate December 22, 1859. Approved by the Governor December 22, 1859.

CHAPTER 997—[No. 2.]

AN ACT concerning Sheriffs and Coroners.

SECTION 1. *Be it enacted by the Senate and House of Representatives of the State of Florida in General Assembly convened*, That any Sheriff or Coroner who shall fail duly to execute and return all process to him directed, shall be subject to a penalty of one hundred dollars for each neglect, to be paid to the party grieved, by order of the Court upon motion and proof that the process was delivered to him twenty days before the sitting of the Court to which the same is returnable, unless such Sheriff or Coroner can show sufficient cause to the Court for his failure at the term next succeeding such order, and such Sheriff or Coroner, for every such neglect of duty to execute and return process delivered to him as aforesaid, shall be further subject to indictment in any Court of record, and, on conviction, shall be fined or imprisoned, at the discretion of the Court. *Penalty for failing to execute & return process.* *Excuse, when may be made.* *Indictment.*

SEC. 2. *Be it further enacted*, That every Sheriff, by himself or his lawful officers or deputies, shall from time to time execute all writs and other process to him legally issued and directed within his county and make due return thereof, under the penalty of forfeiting one hundred dollars for each *Duty of Sheriff to execute & return process.* *Penalty for failure, to whom paid.*

1859.

neglect, where such process shall be delivered to him twenty days before the sitting of the Court to which the same is returnable, to be paid to the party grieved by the order of such Court, upon motion and proof of such delivery, unless such Sheriff can show sufficient cause for such failure or neglect to the Court at the next succeeding term after such **Penalty for false return.** order; and, for every false return, the Sheriff shall forfeit and pay five hundred dollars, one moiety thereof to the party grieved and the other moiety to him or those that will **Action therefor.** sue for the same, to be recovered with costs by action of debt; and, moreover, the said Sheriff shall be further liable to the action of the party grieved for damages.

Criminal cases. SEC. 3. *Be it further enacted*, That this act shall be construed to extend to and include all process in criminal as well as civil cases.

Security of Sh'ff liable. SEC. 4. *Be it further enacted*, That the securities to Sheriff bonds shall be liable to all fines and amercements which shall or may be imposed upon him to the same extent as they are now liable for all other deficiencies in the official duty of Sheriffs.

Repeal. SEC. 5. *Be it further enacted*, That all laws and parts of laws conflicting with the true meaning and intent of this act be and the same are hereby repealed.

Passed the Senate January 13th, 1859. Passed the House of Representatives December 14, 1859. Approved by the Governor December 22, 1859.

CHAPTER 998—[No. 3.]

AN ACT to amend the Attachment Laws of this State.

SECTION 1. *Be it enacted by the Senate and House of Representatives of the State of Florida in General Assembly convened*, That, from and after the passage of this act, **When writ to issue.** writ of attachment, now authorized by statutes of this State to be issued where the debt or demand is due, shall in no case be issued, unless the party applying for the same, or his agent or attorney, shall first make oath in writing, be- **Oath of party applying for.** fore a Justice of the Peace or Clerk of the Circuit Court, as is now provided by law, that the amount of the debt or sum demanded is actually due, and also that he or she has reason to believe the party from whom it is due will fraudulently part with his, her or their property before judgment can be recovered against him, her or them, (as the case may be,) or is actually removing his, her or their property out of the State of Florida, or about to remove it out of the State, or resides beyond the limits thereof, or is actually removing or about to remove out of the State, or absconds or conceals himself or herself, or is secreting his or her property or fraudulently disposing of the same.

Sec. 2. *Be it further enacted*, That all laws and parts of laws inconsistent with the true intent and meaning of this act be and the same are hereby repealed : *Provided*, That nothing herein contained shall affect any proceeding now pending in any of the Courts in this State under the attachment laws now in force.

Repeal.

Proviso.

Passed the House of Representatives December 10, 1859. Passed the Senate December 14, 1859. Approved by the Governor December 20, 1859.

Chapter 999—[No. 4.]

AN ACT to amend the Laws now in force in this State relative to Ejectment Suits.

Section 1. *Be it enacted by the Senate and House of Representatives of the State of Florida in General Assembly convened*, That, from and after the passage of this act, in all actions of ejectment, it shall not be necessary to have any fictitious parties to said suit of ejectment, but the party claiming may bring his suit directly against the party in possession or the one claiming adversely, and the declaration shall only contain a plain statement of the cause of action to entitle the plaintiff to recover the land in controversy, together with mesne profits. Said declaration may be in the following form, to wit :

Fictitious parties abolished.

What declaration to contain.

In the Circuit Court of Florida,   Circuit,
term A. D. 185   County, to wit :

Form of

A B, by his attorney, complains of C D, who has been summoned to answer him in an action of ejectment, for that whereas the defendant is in the possession of a certain tract or parcel of land, situate, lying and being in said county, known and described as follows, to wit: (here describe the land,) containing about   acres, to which said plain-

3

tiff claims title; and the defendant has received the profits of said land since the   day of   A. D.. of the yearly value of   dollars, and refuses to deliver the possession of said land to the said plaintiff or to pay him the profits thereof.

Plea of not guilty, when to put in issue.

Sec. 2. *Be it further enacted*, That the plea of not guilty, put in by the defendant, shall put in issue the title of said land in controversy.

Passed the House of Representatives January 15, 1859. Passed the Senate December 6, 1859. Approved by the Governor December 20, 1859.

CHAPTER 1,000—[No. 5.]

AN ACT to provide for the payment of Constables' fees for summoning Juries of Inquest and attendance on the same.

Fees of Constables.

SECTION 1. *Be it enacted by the Senate and House of Representatives of the State of Florida in General Assembly convened*, That, from and after the passage of this act, the several Constables of this State shall have and receive the sum of twenty-five cents for each and every person summoned by them to serve upon a jury of inquest, and that

Per diem of.

said Constables shall severally receive one dollar and twenty-five cents per day during their actual attendance on the same, to be paid with the costs of the inquest, and paid out of the treasury of the State, as now provided by law.

Repeal.

SEC. 2. *Be it further enacted*, That all laws inconsistent with the same be and the same are hereby repealed.

Passed the Senate December 21, 1858. Passed the House of Representatives December 5, 1859. Approved by the Governor December 19, 1859.

CHAPTER 1,001—[No. 6.]

AN ACT concerning Costs and Fees.

Fees of Commissioners for taking testimony.

SECTION 1. *Be it enacted by the Senate and House of Representatives of the State of Florida in General Assembly convened*, That Commissioners, taking testimony by virtue of any commission issuing from any of the Courts of this State, shall be entitled to five dollars for each witness examined by them, said sum to be divided between the Commissioners, which said sum shall be paid by the party at whose instance the testimony is taken and shall be taxed in the bill of costs.

Sec. 2. *Be it further enacted*, That when any Sheriff shall make a levy by virtue of any execution, he shall be entitled to his commissions at the rate now prescribed by law, notwithstanding the defendant may have paid the debt to the plaintiff or his attorney.

Sheriff levying execution entitled to comm'ns.

Sec. 3. *Be it further enacted*, That if the defendant, in any indictment except indictments for assault and battery, libel or trespass, shall make oath in writing, and the Sheriff of the county where said indictment shall also certify that said defendant is utterly unable to pay the cost of said prosecution, the Court shall order that the said costs as they accrue be taxed against the State, and the Clerk of said Court shall issue certificates against the State for costs due to witnesses summoned by said defendant, in the same manner as if they had been summoned by the State, and shall immediately forward a copy of said order to the Comptroller.

Court may order costs of defendant in criminal cases to be taxed against State, when.

Clerk to issue certificates to witnesses for costs.

To forward copy to Comptroller.

Passed the House of Representatives December 21st, 1859. Passed the Senate December 22, 1859. Approved by the Governor December 22, 1859.

Chapter 1,002—[No. 7.]

AN ACT to extend the time for collecting Taxes in this State.

Section 1. *Be it enacted by the Senate and House of Representatives of the State of Florida in General Assembly convened*, That the time for collecting taxes in this State shall be and is hereby extended from the first day of October to the first day of December in each and every year, and that it shall not be lawful for any Tax-Collector to issue any execution to enforce the payment of taxes until after the said first day of December of the year for which the said taxes are due and unpaid.

Time extended to 1st of December.

Unlawful for Tax-Collector to enforce payment until after.

Sec. 2. *Be it further enacted*, That the several Tax-Assessors and Collectors of this State shall make their returns to the Comptroller on or before the first day of January in each and every year, under the same provisions as are now provided by law.

Returns to be made to Comptroller by first January.

Passed the Senate January 6, 1859. Passed the House of Representatives January 15, 1859. Approved by the Governor December 12, 1859.

CHAPTER 1,003—[No. 8.]

AN ACT to grant retail Licenses in the State of Florida.

License to retail liquor may be issued.

SECTION 1. *Be it enacted by the Senate and House of Representatives of the State of Florida in General Assembly convened,* That from and after the passage of this act, it shall and may be lawful for Licenses to retail Spiritous Liquors in the State of Florida, to be issued upon the payment of one hundred dollars by the party or parties applying for the same.

Tax thereof.

SEC. 2. *Be it further enacted,* That in all other respects except as to the price or amount of tax for said license, the same shall be taken out and issued in the same manner as is now provided by law.

How taken out.

Repeal.

SEC. 3. *Be it further enacted,* That all laws or parts of laws inconsistent herewith, be, and the same are hereby repealed.

Passed the House of Representatives December 15, 1859. Passed the Senate December 19, 1859. Approved by the Governor December 21, 1859.

CHAPTER 1,004—[No. 9.]

AN ACT to amend an act entitled an act to amend an act to establish the Ad Valorem System of Taxation, approved January 15th, 2859.

Act, how amended.

SECTION 1. *Be it enacted by the Senate and House of Representatives of the State of Florida in General Assembly convened* That the fourth line in the seventh section of said act shall be so amended as to insert after the words " every description," in said line, the words " due him."

Passed the House of Representatives December 16th, 1859. Passed the Senate December 22d, 1859. Approved by the Governor December 22d, 1859.

CHAPTER 1,005—[No. 10.]

AN ACT for the protection and disposal of Wrecked and Derelict Goods in the State of Florida.

SECTION 1. *Be it enacted by the Senate and House of Rep-*

reservatives of the State of Florida in General Assembly *convened.* That whenever any wrecked derelict goods shall be found in any County of this State, it shall be the duty of the Judge of Probate for said County to ascertain the amount and situation of the same, and by his written order cause the Sheriff of said county to take charge thereof, and to sell the same at public outcry, after giving reasonable public notice of the time and place of such sale.

Judge of Probate to ascertain amount & situation of goods.

To order Sheriff to sell same.

Notice.

SEC. 2. *Be it further enacted,* That in order to ascertain the quantum of salvage to be paid to the person or persons finding and reporting such wrecked derelict goods, the said Judge of Probate shall appoint two discreet citizens of said county as arbitrators, who shall be authorized, in case of disagreement, to select an umpire, who shall determine the quantum of salvage, not to exceed one half the proceeds of such goods to be paid to the salvors or persons finding and reporting such goods, and the said Judge of Probate shall draw his order upon the Sheriff, who shall pay the same, for the amount so awarded in favor of the said salvors.

Quantum of salvage to be paid person finding, how ascertain'd.

Limitation of.

How paid.

SEC. 3. *Be it further enacted,* That it shall be the duty of said Sheriff to hold the balance of the proceeds of such sale, after paying to the Judge of Probate one per centum of the said balance for his services, and retaining two and one half per centum of the gross amount of said sale for his commissions, for the term of one year and a day, unless the same shall be claimed, and the said claim or claims established within said period, and after the lapse of said period it shall be the duty of said Sheriff to pay the same over to the Register of Public Lands to be by him paid into the Treasury of the School Fund.

Compensation to Judge of Probate and Sheriff.

Unless claim'd within one year balance to whom paid.

SEC. 4. *Be it further enacted,* That any person finding wrecked or derelict goods in any county of this State, who shall fail to report the same to the Judge of Probate for the county wherein the same may be found, shall, upon conviction thereof, before any Justice of the Peace or Circuit Court of this State, be fined in the sum of double the amount of the goods so found, one half of which shall be paid to the party or parties informing and the balance to be paid to the Register, to be by him paid into the Treasury to the School fund.

Fine against person finding wreck'd or derelict goods for not reporting same to Judge of Probate.

To whom paid.

SEC. 5. *Be it further enacted,* That all laws or parts of laws conflicting with this act, be, and the same are hereby repealed.

Repeal.

Passed the House of Representatives December 21st, 1859. Passed the Senate December 22d, 1859. Approved by the Governor December 22d, 1859.

CHAPTER 1,006— [No. 11.]

AN ACT to require Physicians and Surgeons to file certified copies of their Diplomas.

Certified copy of diploma may be filed with Cl'k of Circuit Court in lieu of original.

SECTION 1. *Be it enacted by the Senate and House of Representatives of the State of Florida in General Assembly convened,* That, from and after the passage of this act, any Physician or Surgeon who shall file a certified copy of his Diploma in the office of the Clerk of the Circuit Court of the county in which he may reside, such copy shall be as good and valid, to all intents and purposes, as if the original had been filed, all laws and parts of laws to the contrary notwithstanding.

Passed the House of Representatives December 18, 1859. Passed the Senate December 19, 1859. Approved by the Governor December 21, 1859.

CHAPTER 1,007—[No. 12.]

AN ACT to prevent the unnecessary use of Fire-arms in the State of Florida on Sunday.

Hunting and target shooting on Sunday.

SECTION 1. *Be it enacted by the Senate and House of Representatives of the State of Florida in General Assembly convened,* That from and after the passage of this act, it shall not be lawful for any person or persons within the State of Florida to use fire-arms by hunting game or firing at targets upon Sunday.

Penalty.

SEC. 2. *Be it further enacted by the authority aforesaid,* That any violation of this act shall be deemed a misdemeanor, and the person or persons so offending shall, upon conviction thereof before any justice of the Peace, be punished by a fine of not less than five nor more than twenty-five dollars, or imprisonment not exceeding twenty days.

Passed the House of Representatives December 7, 1859. Passed the Senate December 19, 1859. Approved by the Governor December 22, 1859

AN ACT to allow Spiritous Liquors to be drank where sold.

SECTION 1. *Be it enacted by the Senate and House of Representatives of the State of Florida in General Assembly convened*, That from and after the passage and approval of this act, it shall be lawful for any person residing in the State of Florida, who shall sell spiritous liquors in quantity of one quart and upwards, to permit the same to be drank in the house or houses where the same shall have been sold.

Persons selling liquor in quantity of one quart and over may permit same to be drank where sold.

SEC. 2. *Be it further enacted*, That all laws now in force in this State inconsistent with the provision of this act be and the same are hereby repealed.

Repeal.

Passed the House of Representatives December 9, 1859. Passed the Senate December 14, 1859. Approved by the Governor December 20, 1859.

CHAPTER 1,009—[No. 14.]

AN ACT to amend the law allowing appeals from the decisions of the Boards of County Commissioners in this State.

SECTION 1. *Be it enacted by the Senate and House of Representatives of the State of Florida in General Assembly convened*, That the statutes authorizing appeals from the orders and decisions of the Boards of County Commissioners of the several counties of this State, shall be so amended that the appeal may be taken at any time within four days after the adjournment of the Board passing the same.

Appeal may be taken within four days from adjournment.

SEC. 2. *Be it further enacted*, That the bond required of the aggrieved party so appealing by the act to which this is an amendment, shall be approved by the Judge of Probate as ex-officio President of the Board.

Appeal bond, by whom approved.

SEC. 3. *Be it further enacted*, That the Circuit Courts of this State, to which any appeal may hereafter be taken from the decisions of the Boards of County Commissioners, shall proceed to try said appeal upon the merits *de novo*.

Appeal to be tried de novo.

SEC. 4. *Be it further enacted*, That all laws or parts of

Repeal.

laws conflicting with this act be and the same are hereby repealed.

Passed the Senate December 7, 1859. Passed the House of Representatives December 12, 1859. Approved by the Governor 19, 1859.

CHAPTER 1,010—[No. 15.]

AN ACT for the payment of the Florida volunteers called into service under the requisition of the Governor of this State for services rendered previous to their being mustered in, during the years 1855-'6.

SECTION 1. *Be it enacted by the Senate and House of Representatives of the State of Florida in General Assembly convened,* That the Comptroller of this State be, and he is hereby required to audit and allow, and the Treasurer of this State is hereby required to pay, upon warrant from the Comptroller, all amounts due Volunteer Companies organized and who actually did service under the instructions of the Governor of this State, dated the first day of January A. D. eighteen hundred and fifty six, previous to the time of such Companies being regularly mustered into service.

Comptroller to audit and Treasurer to pay amounts due to companies.

SEC. 2. *Be it further enacted,* That said Companies shall be paid pro rata, and upon the same terms for service previously rendered by them, that they have been paid and that has been allowed and audited to them for services rendered subsequently to being mustered in.

Payment to be made pro rata.

SEC. 3. *Be it further enacted,* That the Comptroller, before he shall audit or allow any accounts, shall require first, due proof of such requisition as aforesaid by the Governor of this State; second, due and satisfactory proof of organization; third, due and satisfactory proof of services actually performed.

Comptroller, before auditing, to require proof, &c.

SEC. 4. *Be it further enacted,* That the same shall be paid by and in accordance with the terms and provisions of the act approved January 7, A. D., 1853, entitled an act to provide for the payment of Captains Sparkman. Parkers and other volunteer companies for service in the year 1849, and also of an act to provide for the payment of the debts of the State, approved December 27th, 1856, and that upon due proof as herein aforesaid stated. the Governor of this State is authorized to provide for the payment of said Companies in the same mode and manner as provided by the said act. ap-

Payment, upon what terms to be made.

Governor authorized to provide for.

proved seventh day of January, A. D. 1853; or that the same may and shall be paid out of any money in the Treasury not otherwise appropriated.

Or may be paid out of Treasury.

Sec. 5. *Be it further enacted*, That all acts and parts of acts inconsistent herewith are hereby repealed.

Repeal.

Passed the House of Representatives December 8, 1859. Passed the Senate December 17, 1859. Approved by the Governor December 20, 1859.

Chapter 1,011—[No. 16.]

AN ACT to amend an act entitled an act to establish Common Schools and to repeal certain acts in relation thereto, approved January 1st, 1853.

Section 1. *Be it enacted by the Senate and House of Representatives of the State of Florida in General Assembly convened*, That the Superintendent of Schools for the State, upon demand, shall pay the amount of School money apportioned annually to each county to the Judge of Probate of the county, to be appropriated as required by law.

Am't of School money apportioned to each county, by wh'm paid and how appropriated.

Sec. 2. *Be it further enacted*, That the Judge of Probate of each county, when any School shall be established by the County Commissioners, may contract with any person whom the Trustees of the School shall in writing recommend as a Teacher.

Judge of Probate may contract with teacher.

Passed the House of Representatives January 14, 1859. Passed the Senate December 20, 1859. Approved by the Governor December 22, 1859.

Chapter 1,012—[No. 17.]

AN ACT to allow Additional Compensation to County Commissioners.

Section 1. *Be it enacted by the Senate and House of Representatives of the State of Florida in General Assembly convened*, That every County Commissioner shall be entitled to receive from the county treasury of his county ten cents per mile going to and returning from his place of residence to the Court House or place of holding Commissioners' Court.

Mileage to Co. Commission'rs.

Passed the House of Representatives December 6, 1859. Passed the Senate December 9, 1859. Approved by the Governor December 19, 1859.

CHAPTER 1,013—[No. 18.]

AN ACT in relation to Courts of Probate in this State.

Courts of Probate to be alw'ys open. SECTION 1. *Be it enacted by the Senate and House of Representatives of the State of Florida in General Assembly convened,* That from and after the passage of this act the Courts of Probate in this State shall not be held at any particular stated times or periods, but shall be held and considered at all times open for the transaction of business in relation to estates of deceased persons.

Returns of ex'rs, administrators & guardians, when may be made. SEC. 2. *Be it further enacted,* That executors, administrators and guardians may make their annual returns at any time before the first day of June in each and every year.

Forfeiture of commissions for failure to make returns. SEC. 3. *Be it further enacted,* That every executor, administrator and guardian who shall fail to make the returns required of him by law by the first day of June, as provided in the second section of this act, shall forfeit all commissions on the returns so to be made.

Appeals from Courts of Probate to be tried de novo. SEC. 4. *Be it further enacted.* That all appeals from the decisions, orders or decrees of the Courts of Probate to the Circuit Courts, as now provided for by law, shall be tried **And by jury.** by the said Circuit Courts upon the merits *de novo,* and in all cases the facts shall be tried by a jury, as in original suits.

Repeal. SEC. 5. *Be it further enacted,* That all acts and parts of acts conflicting with this act be and the same are hereby repealed.

Passed the Senate December 8, 1859. Passed the House of Representatives December 15, 1859. Approved by the Governor December 22, 1859.

CHAPTER 1,014—[No. 19.]

AN ACT in relation to Records.

Clerks of Circuit Court to make reversed index. SECTION 1. *Be it enacted by the Senate and House of Representatives of the State of Florida in General Assembly convened,* That the several Clerks of the Circuit Courts shall make, alphabetically arranged, a reversed Index of the names of the contracting parties to every deed of conveyance or instrument of writing admitted to the records of conveyances, mortgages and agreements, and the said clerks shall be entitled to demand and receive five cents for making every such reversed Index.

Passed the House of Representatives December 8th, 1859. Passed the Senate December 22d, 1859. Approved by the Governor December 22d, 1859.

CHAPTER 1,015—[No. 20.]

AN ACT to repeal in part the 24th section of the act entitled an act to provide for and encourage a liberal system of Internal Improvements in this State, approved January 6, 1855.

SECTION 1. *Be it enacted by the Senate and House of Representatives of the State of Florida in General Assembly convened*, That so much of the 24th section of the act to which this is an amendment as provides that no branch road shall be made from the main line of railroad to the Northern boundary line of this State to a point West of the Alapaha river, without the consent of all the companies owning the main line of road between the waters of Escambia Bay and the Florida Railroad, and without the approval of the Trustees of the Internal Improvement Fund, be and the same is hereby repealed.

Repeal.

Passed the Senate December 17, 1859. Passed the House of Representatives December 22, 1859. Approved by the Governor December 22, 1859.

CHAPTER 1,016—[No. 21.]

AN ACT concerning Roads.

SECTION 1. *Be it enacted by the Senate and House of Representatives of the State of Florida in General Assembly convened*, That if any Commissioner of Roads, or Overseer of Roads, in this State shall fail faithfully to discharge any of the duties imposed upon them respectively by any law of this State, the person so offending shall be liable to indictment, and, on conviction, shall be punished by a fine not exceeding one hundred dollars, at the discretion of the Court.

Indictment of commissioner & overseer of roads for failure of duty.

Fine.

SEC. 2. *Be it further enacted*, That Physicians and Sur-

Physicians and

S'rgeons exempt from road duty. geons in actual practice be and they are hereby exempted from road duty, except as to slaves owned by them.

Passed the House of Representatives December 12, 1859.　Passed the Senate December 19, 1859.　Approved l y the Governor December 21, 1859.

CHAPTER 1,017—[No. 22.]

AN ACT in relation to the Boundary Line now being run between this State and Georgia.

Boundary line declared.

SECTION 1. *Be it enacted by the Senate and House of Representatives of the State of Florida in General Assembly convened,* That the line now being run by B. F. Whitner, Jr., on the part of Florida, and G. J. Orr, on the part of Georgia, be and the same is hereby recognized and declared to be the permanent boundary line between the two States, so soon as the same shall be permanently marked by said Surveyors:

Proviso. *Provided,* The said line at its Eastern terminus does not depart from or miss Ellicott's Mound more than one-fourth of a mile or twenty chains.

Titles to land derived from Georgia confirmed.

SEC. 2. *Be it further enacted,* That the titles of *bona fide* holders of land under any grant from the State of Georgia, which land may fall within this State by the foregoing line, are hereby confirmed and conveyed to said holders, so far as any right may accrue to this State:

Proviso. *Provided,* Nothing herein shall apply to lands to which citizens of this State may claim title South of what is known as the McNeil line.

Passed the Senate December 22, 1859.　Passed the House of Representatives December 22, 1859.　Approved by the Governor December 22, 1859.

CHAPTER 1,018—[No. 23.]

AN ACT to provide for the payment of Costs by Plaintiffs, in certain cases, in the Western Judicial Circuit.

SECTION 1. *Be it enacted by the Senate and House of Representatives of the State of Florida in General Assembly convened,* That from and after the passage of this act, whenever the plaintiff or plaintiffs in any action of debt shall recover any sum not exceeding fifty dollars, exclusive of interest and costs, in any Circuit Court in the Western Judicial Circuit of this State, except on *certiorari* or when the amount of the original debt is reduced by plea or offset, then the said plaintiff or plaintiffs shall not recover any costs against the defendant, but shall pay the whole costs of the suit.

Costs, when to be paid by plaintiffs.

 Passed the Senate December 9, 1859. Passed the House of Representatives December —, 1859. Approved by the Governor December 21, 1859.

CHAPTER 1,019.—[No. 24.]

AN ACT to authorize the Board of Education of the State Seminary West of the Suwannee to confer Collegiate Degrees.

SECTION 1. *Be it enacted by the Senate and House of Representatives of the State of Florida in General Assembly convened*, That after the first day of January, 1860, the Board of Education of the State Seminary located at Tallahassee shall have the power to confer Collegiate Degrees.

Collegiate degrees may be conferred.

Passed the House of Representatives December 19, 1859. Passed the Senate December 19, 1859. Approved December 22, 1859.

CHAPTER 1,020.—[No. 25.]

AN ACT to authorize the Trustees of the Internal Improvement Fund to clean out the channel of the Ocklawaha river in this State for the purpose of improving the navigation of the same, and other purposes.

SECTION 1. *Be it enacted by the Senate and House of Representatives of the State of Florida in General Assembly convened*, That the Trustees of the Internal Improvement Fund are hereby authorized and empowered to contract for the cleaning out of the channel of the Ocklawaha river from its mouth to lake Ahapopka and also the branch to Silver Spring in this State, for the purpose of draining the swamp lands contiguous thereto, and for improving the navigation of the same.

Trustees authorized to contract for clearing out channel of Ocklawaha river.

SEC. 2. *Be it further enacted*, That the said Trustees of the Internal Improvement Fund are hereby authorized to

May pledge Swamp lands on the river of the

value thereof in money for clearing out channel.

Proviso.

pledge so much of the swamp lands as lie upon the Ockla-waha river, or the value thereof in money, as in their opinion may be necessary for the purpose hereinbefore mentioned : *Provided,* That the same does not conflict with the main object of the trust, the interest of the several railroads now being built in the State, and the interest of the holders of the Internal Improvement bonds.

Passed the Senate December 8, 1859. Passed the House of Representatives December 20, 1859. Approved December 22, 1859.

CHAPTER 1,021—[No. 26.]

AN ACT in relation to the Gulf City and Interior Railroad Company, and the Pensacola and Georgia Railroad Company.

Preamble.

WHEREAS, on the 15th January, A. D., 1859, two bills having in view the construction of a Railroad from the vicinity of Tallahassee to the waters of the Bay of Apalachicola, or St. George's Sound, were approved by the Governor of this State and have been published among the acts of the Legislature, then in session, which said acts, as they in fact and in truth passed both Houses of the General Assembly, are in the words and figures, as follows, to-wit : " An act to incorporate the Gulf City and Interior Railroad Company."

Commissioners to open books of subscription.

SECTION 1. *Be it enacted by the Senate and House of Representatives of the State of Florida in General Assembly convened,* That Isaac R. Harris, Samuel B. Stephens and D. P. Holland of Gadsden County, Joseph Chaires, R. A. Shine, W. G. M. Davis and M. P. Ellis of Leon County, D. Ladd, Wakulla County, and R. J. Floyd, D. K. Dodge, Thomas Orman and D. J. Day, of Franklin County, or any two or more of them, are hereby appointed Commissioners to open books and receive subscriptions in their respective Counties for stock in a Railroad to be constructed from the waters of Apalachicola Bay, or St. George's Sound, to a point south of the line of Railroad from Pensacola to Jacksonville and Fernandina, and not more than one mile distant from the City of Tallahassee, or to a point of junction on the Tal-

Books, when and how long to be kept open.

lahassee Railroad between St. Marks and Tallahassee, and said Commissioners shall open said books after the expira-

tion of sixty days from the passage of this act, and shall keep
the same open for the space of sixty days; and said commissioners shall give notice, in a newspaper published in
Tallahassee, of the time and place when and where said books
are to be opened, and in case of an excessive subscription
over and above the sum herein fixed for the capital stock of
said Company, the said Commissioners shall have power to Excessive subscription to be
reduced pro rata
reduce said subscriptions pro rata, so as to bring the same
down to the amount of said capital.

Sec. 2. *Be it further enacted*, That the said Railroad
shall be located at some point on the Bay of Apalachicola
or St. George's Sound, to be determined as hereinafter provided, and from thence to a point south of the line of Railroad from Pensacola to Jacksonville and Fernandina, and
not more than one mile distant from the city of Tallahassee,
or to a point or junction on the Tallahassee Railroad between
St. Marks and Tallahassee: *Provided*, That the said Rail- Location not to
violate v e s t e d
rights or conflict
w i t h Internal
Imp. law.
road shall not be located or constructed in any way or manner in violation of the vested rights of any other corporation,
or in conflict with any of the provisions and guarantees of
the act entitled an act to provide for and encourage a liberal
system of internal improvement in this State, approved January 6th, 1855; *Provided also*, That before said Railroad
Company shall fix and establish the terminus of said Road
at any point on the Bay of Apalachicola or St. George's
Sound, the location of said terminus shall be approved by a
vote of two-thirds of the votes of said company, at a stockholder's meeting, and shall also be assented to by the Board
of Internal Improvements of this State after a full examina-
tion of all the proofs submitted to them as to the suitable-
ness of such proposed terminus for the purposes of commerce,
and upon the said Board being convinced from the evidence
before them that the place proposed for such terminus is
the best fitted by nature for a seaport town, having the best
water, safest anchorage, and greatest facility for construction
of wharves and piers for shipping at the smallest expense
of any other point or place, lying and being on the waters
aforesaid.

Sec. 3. *Be it further enacted*, That the capital stock of
said Company at its commencement, shall be Five Hundred
Thousand Dollars, to be divided into shares of one hundred
dollars each; but said Company shall have the power to increase such capital to one million of dollars, if such increase

shall be found necessary to the completion or successful operation of said Railroad.

Sec. 4. *Be it further enacted*, That as soon as one hundred thousand dollars shall have been subscribed to the capital stock of said company, the subscribers of said stock, their successors and assigns, shall be, and they are hereby declared to be incorporated into a company by the name of the Gulf City and Interior Railroad company, and by that name shall be capable in law of purchasing, holding, leasing, selling and conveying real, personal and mixed property so far as shall be necessary for the purpose of this incorporation ; and by said incorporated name may sue and be sued, plead and be impleaded, answer and be answered unto, in any court of law or equity in this State, or elsewhere, and to have and use a common seal, and the same to alter or amend at pleasure, to frame such by-laws, rules and ordinances for the good government of said company as to them may seem proper, and generally do all things necessary to carry into effect fully and completely the object of this act.

Sec. 5. *Be it further enacted*, That as soon as one hundred thousand dollars shall have been subscribed, the commissioners hereby appointed shall call a meeting of the subscribers, at such time and place as they may appoint, and at such meeting the said subscribers, or a majority of them in value, shall elect nine directors by ballot, to manage the affairs of said company, and the commissioners aforesaid, or or any three or more of them, shall be judges of the said first election of Directors, and the Directors thus chosen shall elect (from) among themselves a President of said Company, and allow him such compensation as they may think proper ; and on all occasions whenever a vote of stockholders shall be necessary to be taken, each stockholder shall be allowed one vote for every share owned by him or her, and on which all the instalments called for have been paid, and all voting shall be in proportion to the amount paid, and not the amount subscribed to said stock, and any stockholder may depute any other person to vote and act for him or her, as his or her proxy.

Sec. 6. *Be it further enacted*, That the President and Directors of said company shall be chosen annually by the stockholders of said company, and if any vacancy shall occur by death, resignation or otherwise, of any President or Directors before the year for which they were elected shall

Side notes:

Body corporate.

Name.

May hold property.

May sue and be sued.

Common seal.

By-laws, &c.

Meet'g of stockholders to be called by Commissioners, when

To elect directors.

Directors to elect President.

His compensation.

Vote of stockholders according to amount paid in.

May act by proxy.

President and directors to be chosen annually

Vacancies, how filled.

have expired, such vacancy shall be filled by the President and Directors or a majority of them, and that the President and Directors shall hold their office until their successors are chosen and qualified, shall have power to call meetings of stockholders at any time, and a majority of stockholders shall have power to remove the President or any Directors, and to fill all vacancies occasioned by removal at pleasure.

To hold office till successors chosen & qualified.

May call meeting of stockholders, who may remove and fill vacancies.

SEC. 7. *Be it further enacted,* That the said President and Directors, or a majority of them, may appoint all such officers, engineers, agents or servants whatsoever as they may deem necessary to carry on the business of said company, dismiss them at pleasure, and a majority of them shall determine the compensation of all officers, engineers and servants of said company ; shall have power to pass all by-laws which they may deem necessary and proper for exercising all the powers vested in this company for carrying into effect the objects of this act ; *Provided only,* That such by-laws shall not be contrary to the laws of this State or the United States, and said President and Directors, or a majority of them, are empowered to borrow money to carry into effect the object of this act, to issue certificates or other evidence of such loan, and to pledge the property of said company for the payment of the same with interest.

President and Directors may appoint or dismiss all officers.

May fix compensation.

May pass by-laws.

Proviso.

May borrow money.

Issue certificates of debt. Pledge property of Company.

SEC. 8. *Be it further enacted,* That the said President and Directors shall have power to require the stockholders of said company to pay such instalments on their respective shares of stock in said company, and at such time as they may think best for the interest of said company, and upon failure or refusal of any stockholder to pay the instalment required on his, her or their stock, in pursuance of any call made by said President and Directors as aforesaid, said President and Directors may, upon giving thirty days notice, proceed to sell at public sale the share or shares of said stock owned by said stockholder or such part as they may think proper, to the highest bidder, and if upon sale of the shares of stock owned by said defaulting stockholder, said stock be sold for more than the amount due upon instalment as above mentioned, the excess, after deducting an accruing interest and the necessary expenses of sale, shall be paid over to said defaulting stockholder.

President and Directors may call for instalments of stock.

May sell shares of stock for payment.

Excess of sale to be paid to defaulting stockholder.

SEC. 9. *Be it further enacted,* That the President and Directors of said company are hereby authorized to contract for and receive conveyances of land, stone, lumber and wood

President and Directors may receive conveyances of land,&c.

5

Proceedings when no agreement with own'r upon the price, or owner be an infant or *non compos mentis.*

which may be necessary or required in the construction of said Railroad, and when the owner and company cannot agree upon the price, or when the owner is an infant, non-resident or *non compos mentis,* then it shall be lawful for the President and Directors of said company to apply to the sheriff of the county in which said land or other property may be situated, who shall summon a jury of *seven* disinterested freeholders, a majority of whom shall be authorized to assess the damages and return their award or judgment to the next term of the Circuit Court for the county in which said

Judgment and execution thereupon.

land or other property may be situated, which shall be entered by the Clerk as the judgment of the Court, and execution may issue thereupon for the amount of said judgment and costs ; *Provided always,* That if either party shall, upon the return thereof, be dissatisfied, they may, upon filing

Appeal.

bond with a good and sufficient security, in such sum as the Court may order, be allowed an appeal to the next term of

Trial *de novo.*

the Circuit Court, when said case shall stand for trial *de novo ; Provided also,* That thirty day's notice shall have

Notice of app'al.

been given to the opposite party, issued by the Clerk of the Court and served by the sheriff of the County.

SEC. 10. *Be it further enacted,* That the jurors sum-

Oath of jury.

moned as aforesaid, shall, (before proceeding to the discharge of the duties herein required) take an oath or affirmation, which the sheriff is hereby authorized to administer, to the effect that they will well and truly inquire into, and to the best of their judgment assess the damages accruing to the owner or owners of such lands or materials, or lands and materials, by means of the proposed construction.

SEC. 11. *Be it further enacted,* That the said lands or

On payment of amount assessed land, &c., to enure to comp'y.

other property so condemned and estimated as aforesaid, shall enure to and become the property of said company for the purpose aforesaid, upon payment by the said company of the amount assessed by said jury to the party claiming damages on account of the construction of said road through said lands, or for such other property ; *Provided,* That said

Proviso.

work shall in no case be delayed on account of the proceedings had as aforesaid.

Forfeiture to Company for injury or obstruction to road.

SEC. 12. *Be it further enacted,* That in case any person shall wilfully injure or obstruct in any degree the said road or roads, he shall forfeit and pay to the President and Directors of said company three times the amount of all damages they may sustain in consequence thereof, to be sued for and

·recovered in the same manner as provided by law for individuals in like cases; and on complaint to any magistrate within whose jurisdiction such offence shall be committed, it Offender to be bound for good behavior to Magistrate. shall be the duty of such magistrate to bind the person or persons so offending, with sufficient security for his or their good behavior, for a period of not less than one year, and Indictment and penalty against. such offender shall also be subject to indictment, and shall be sentenced, at the discretion of the Court, to be imprisoned not less than three nor more than six months.

SEC. 13. *Be it further enacted*, That in the construction of said railroad the President and Directors of said Company shall in no manner obstruct any public road now Company not to obstruct public road. established, but shall provide convenient passages to travel over said road.

SEC. 14. *Be it further enacted*, That payments of the subscription to the stock in said railroad, except the first ten Payments on stock (except 1st 10 p'r cent.) may be made in materials, labor,&c. per cent., which shall be paid to the Commissioners in cash at the time of subscribing, may be made in materials, labor, provisions and all and everything necessary for the construction of said road which the Board of Directors, at their discretion, may deem expedient to accept. All moneys re- Money receiv'd by Commiss'ers to be paid to Directors. ceived by the Commissioners for subscriptions to said stock shall be paid over by them to the Directors of said Company, when elected and organized.

SEC. 15. *Be it further enacted*, That after the comple- President and Directors may lay and collect tolls. tion of the said road, or any part thereof, the said President and Directors may lay and collect tolls from all persons, property, merchandize and other commodities transported thereon: *Provided*, The net profit of said road shall not Proviso. exceed twenty-five per cent. per annum.

SEC. 16. *Be it further enacted*, That the General Assem- Reservation to Gen'l Assembly to authorize construction of oth'r roads. bly reserve the right and power to authorize the construction of any railroad to cross the one authorized in this act, at any point the General Assembly may think proper.

SEC. 17. *Be it further enacted*, That nothing in this act Banking privileges and paper for circulation prohibited. shall be so construed as to confer upon said Company any right to exercise the powers of a Banking Company, or to issue any description of paper or evidence of debt intended as circulation.

SEC. 18. *Be it further enacted*, That said Company here- Road to be commenced and be completed. by incorporated shall commence the building of said road within five years and complete the same within fifteen years from the passage of this act.

Company may extend road to Apalachicola river.

SEC. 19. *Be it further enacted*, That said Company shall have the privilege of extending their road from its terminus, on the waters of the Bay of Apalachicola or St. George's Sound, hereafter to be fixed and selected in the manner before provided, to the river of Apalachicola, in Franklin county, or to the city of Apalachicola, by the most direct and practicable route to said city.

Privileges conferred to be used subject to exceptions.

SEC. 20. *Be it further enacted*, That the powers and privileges herein conferred upon the said Gulf City and Interior Railroad Company are to be used and enjoyed subject to the following exception: If the amendment to the charter of the Pensacola and Georgia Railroad Company, passed at this session of the General Asssembly, become a law and be accepted by said Company within six months from the passage of this act, said Gulf City and Interior Railroad Company shall not commence the construction of their road under this act before the expiration of twelve months after the passage thereof, unless with the consent and agreement of the said Pensacola and Georgia Railroad Company.

AN ACT to amend an act to incorporate the Pensacola and Georgia Railroad Company.

Pensacola and Geo. R. R. Co. empowered to build road to Quincy and to Gulf of Mexico.

SECTION 1. *Be it enacted by the Senate and House of Representatives of the State of Florida in General Assembly convened*, That the act incorporating the Pensacola and Georgia Railroad Company is hereby amended, and that said Company be and is hereby empowered to build a branch road from Quincy, Tallahassee, or from some point on the Tallahassee Railroad between Tallahassee and St. Marks, to the Gulf of Mexico, in the county of Franklin, or

Terminus when to be located.

the adjacent bays, harbors or rivers in or North of said county, the terminus of said road to be hereafter located by said Company.

Branch roads to Georgia line.

SEC. 2. *Be it further enacted*, That said Company be and is in like manner empowered to build a road from its main line to the Georgia line, in Hamilton county, East of the Alapaha river, and a road from Quincy, in Gadsden county, or its vicinity, to the Georgia line, in said county of Gadsden.

Branch roads to be assented to by other Companies.

SEC. 3. *Be it further enacted*, That neither of the roads mentioned in the second section of this act shall be built without the assent of the several Railroad Companies having the right to object thereto by virtue of the provisions of an act to provide for and encourage a liberal system of Internal Improvements in this State, approved January 6th, 1855.

SEC. 4. *Be it further enacted,* That the terminus of said road on the Gulf of Mexico, in the county of Franklin, or the adjacent bays, harbors or rivers in or North of said county, shall, before it be finally located and adopted, be approved by a majority in interest of two-thirds of the stock, at a stockholders' meeting, and shall also be approved by the Board of Internal Improvements of this State in the mode and manner provided in and by the second section of the act incorporating the Gulf City and Interior Railroad Company passed at this session of the General Assembly.

Terminus of road on Gulf of Mexico, how approved.

AND WHEREAS, Serious and important mistakes and omissions have occurred in the enrollment of said Gulf City and Interior Railroad bill,

Preamble.

Be it therefore enacted by the Senate and House of Representatives of the State of Florida in General Assembly convened, That said bills, as hereinbefore stated and set forth, are and the same are hereby declared to be the acts which passed the Legislature in January A. D., 1859, and are hereby re-enacted and given the force and validity of law.

Declaration as to the acts which passed in January, 1859.

Re-enactment.

Passed the House of Representatives December 14, 1859. Passed the Senate December 19, 1859. Approved by the Governor December 22, 1859.

CHAPTER 1,022—[No. 27.]

AN ACT to incorporate the Apalachicola and New Orleans Steam Navigation Company.

SECTION 1. *Be it enacted by the Senate and House of Representatives of the State of Florida in General Assembly convened,* That John D. Atkins, Joseph L. Dunham, H. R. Taylor, John C. Maclay, Benjamin Elison, William T. Wood and George Buckman, citizens of the United States and of this State, and such other persons as now are and may be hereafter associated with them, not less than ten in number, of whom at least five shall be residents of this

1859.

Body corporate.

Name.

May sue and be sued.

State, shall be and are hereby constituted and declared to be a body politic and corporate, by the name and style of the Apalachicola and New Orleans Steam Navigation Company, and by that name they and their successors and assigns shall be capable in law of suing and being sued, plead and being impleaded, answering and being answered unto, defending and being defended in all Courts, tribunals and places whatsoever; and shall have power to adopt,

Common seal.

make and use a common seal, and the same at pleasure to change, alter and amend; and they and their successors and

May purchase and hold property. steamers & vessels, &c.

assigns, by the same manner and style, shall be capable of purchasing. holding and conveying any property, real or personal, any steamer or steamers, vessel or vessels, barges or boats of any kind or description whatever, necessary or expedient to carry out and fulfil the object and objects of said corporation.

Capital stock.

SEC. 2. *Be it further enacted*, That the capital stock of said Company shall be one hundred and twenty thousand

Transferable according to by-laws.

dollars, divided into shares of five hundred dollars each, transferrable in such manner and under such restrictions as the said coporation by their by-laws may require and direct.

SEC. 3. *Be it further enacted*, That the above named

Books of subscription to be opened.

persons, or a majority of them, may open books to receive subscription to the capital stock of said corporation at such time or times and place or places as they, or a majority of

On payment of 30 per cent. of stock to give notice of meeting of stockholders to choose directors.

them, may think proper, and, as soon as thirty per centum upon the capital stock shall be subscribed and paid in, to give notice for a meeting of the stockholders to choose five directors from among said stockholders, three of whom, at least, shall be citizens of the State of Florida, and such

When & where and how.

election shall be made at the time and place appointed by such of the stockholders as shall attend for that pur-

Each share entitled to one vote

pose, either in person or by proxy, each share of the capital stock entitling the holder thereof to one vote;

Corporators to be inspectors of first election.

and the said above-named persons, or a majority of them, shall be inspectors of the first election of directors of said corporation and shall certify under their hands

Certificates of election.
Books to be delivered to directors.
Who may keep them open for further subscriptions.

the names of those persons duly elected, and shall deliver over the subscription books to the said directors, who may keep the same open, by a vote of the majority of stockholders, for further subscription, if the same be deemed expedient, until the entire amount of capital stock shall be subscribed, and each stockholder so subscribing after the organization of the said corporation as aforesaid shall be bound by said election and organization until the next annual election in course, as is hereinafter provided, when he shall be entitled to vote as the original stockholders.

New subscribers to be bound by first election.

SEC. 4. *Be it further enacted*, That there shall be an annual meeting of the stockholders of said corporation, at such time and place as the said corporation may provide by its by-laws, for the purpose of electing directors, and that the time of holding the first meeting of the directors under the said first election shall be fixed by the said directors, or a majority of them, and the directors chosen at said election, or at the annual elections to be afterwards held, shall, as soon as may be after every subsequent election, choose out of their number a President; and in case of the death, resignation or removal of the President or any director, such vacancy or vacancies may be filled for the remainder of the year wherein they may happen by the said remaining directors, or a majority of them; and in case of the absence of the President, the said directors, or a majority of them, may appoint a President *pro tem.*, who shall exercise such powers and functions as the by-laws of said corporation may provide.

Annual meeting of stockholders.

Directors to fix time of their first meeting.

Shall choose a President.

May fill vacancies.

May appoint President pro tem.

SEC. 5. *Be it further enacted*, That the said directors, or a majority of them, shall elect, simultaneously with the President and annually, a suitable person, other than a director, who shall discharge the duties of Secretary and Treasurer of said corporation, who shall be a stockholder in the same.

Directors to elect Secretary and Treasurer.

Must be a stockholder.

SEC. 6. *Be it further enacted*, That in case it should happen that an election of directors should not be made when, pursuant to this act, it should be had, the said corporation shall not by reason thereof be dissolved, but such election shall be held at any other time, and the directors previously elected shall continue as directors until a new election shall be had ; a majority of said directors of said corporation to transact all business of said corporation, and they shall have power to call in the capital stock of said Company by such instalments as they may deem advisable, giving thirty days notice thereof to the said stockholders by advertisement in some newspaper or newspapers ; and in case of the non-payment of said instalment, the stockholder so failing to pay his instalment within ten days after the same becomes due, shall forfeit his share or shares and the amount before paid to the corporation.

No dissolution because of failure to elect.

Directors to continue in office until new elect'n

Majority may act

May call in capital stock.

Notice.

Forfeiture for non-payment of stock.

SEC. 7. *Be it further enacted*, That the said Company shall have liberty to transport passengers, goods, wares, merchandize and all other lawful things whatsoever, and of every description, in vessels propelled by steam or otherwise, and in boats, barges, lighters and in all other conveyances by water, between such points and to such places as the said directors, or a majority of them, may designate; and the said directors, or a majority of them, may from time to time appoint such captains, commanders, agents and all other officers and employees as to them may seem proper and necessary for the interests of said corporation.

SEC. 8. *Be it further enacted*, That the directors of the said Company, or a majority of them, shall settle and adjust the books and accounts of said corporation at least once every year and submit a detailed statement of the affairs thereof to the stockholders at their annual meeting, and declare and pay over such dividend of the actual profits thereof as the condition of the said Company may justify; and the stockholders shall have power to adopt such by-laws for the government of said Company as they may deem proper, not inconsistent with this charter or the laws of the State of Florida.

SEC. 9. *Be it further enacted*, That the said directors, or a majority of them, shall have power to exact from the Treasurer or any other officer of said Company a bond, in such sum as they may deem proper, conditioned for the faithful performance of the duties of his said office.

SEC. 10. *Be it further enacted*, That the private property of the stockholders in said Company shall only be liable for the debts, liabilities and obligations of said Company *pro rata*, according to the amount of stock owned by each stockholder.

Passed the Senate December 15, 1859. Passed the House of Representatives December 17, 1859. Approved by the Governor December 21, 1859.

CHAPTER 1,023—[No. 28.]

AN ACT to incorporate the Apalachicola and Columbus Steamboat Company.

SECTION 1. *Be it enacted by the Senate and House of Representatives of the State of Florida in General As-*

[margin notes:]
Company may transport pass'n-gers, goods, &c.

Vessels.

Directors. May appoint Captains, offic'rs &c.

Books & acc'ts to be adjusted annually & submitted to stock-holders.

Dividends to be paid.

Stockholders may adopt by-laws.

Directors may require bond from officers, &c.

Stockholders liable for debts pro rata.

sembly convened, That John D. Atkins, Joseph L. Dunham, William J. McAlister, George Buckman, William H. Young, Collin Gardner and Richard G. Porter, citizens of the United States and of this State, and such other persons as now are and may be hereafter associated with them, not less than ten in number, of whom at least five shall be residents of this State, shall be and are hereby constituted and declared to be a body politic and corporate, by the name and style of the Apalachicola and Columbus Steamboat Company, and by that name they and their successors and assigns shall be capable, in law, of suing and being sued, plead and being impleaded, answering and being answered unto, defending and being defended in all Courts, tribunals and places whatsoever, and shall have power to adopt, make and use a common seal and the same at pleasure change, alter and amend; and they and their successors and assigns, by the same name and style, shall be capable of purchasing, holding and conveying any property, real or personal, any steamboat or steamers, vessel or vessels, barges or boats of any kind or descriptions whatever, necessary or expedient to carry out and fulfil the object and objects of said corporation.

Body corporate.

Name.

May sue and be sued.

Common seal.

May purchase and hold property, steamers & vessels, &c.

SEC. 2. *Be it further enacted*, That the capital stock of said Company shall be one hundred and fifty thousand dollars, divided into shares of one thousand dollars each, transferrable in such manner and under such restrictions as the said corporation, by their by-laws, may require and direct.

Capital stock.

Transferable according to by-laws.

SEC. 3. *Be it further enacted*, That the above-named persons, or a majority of them, may open books to receive subscriptions to the capital stock of said corporation at such time or times and place or places as they, or a majority of them, may think proper, and, as soon as twenty per centum upon the capital stock shall be subscribed and paid in, to give notice for a meeting of the stockholders, to choose five Directors from amongst said stockholders, three of whom, at least, shall be citizens of the State of Florida, and such election shall be made at the time and place appointed by such of the stockholders as shall attend for that purpose, either in person or by proxy, each share of the capital stock entitling the holder thereof to one vote; and the said above named persons, or a majority of them, shall be inspectors of the first election of Directors of said corporation, and shall certify under their hands the names of those persons duly

Books of subscription to bo opened.

On payment of 20 per cent. of stock to give notice of meeting of stockholders to choose directors.

When & where and how.

Each share entitled to one vote

Corporators to be inspectors of first election.

6

1859.

Certificates of election.

Books to be delivered to directors.

Who may keep them open for further subscriptions.

New subscribers to be bound by first election.

Annual meeting of stockholders.

Directors to fix time of their first meeting.

Shall choose a President.

May fill vacancies.

Vacancies, how filled.

May appoint President pro tem.

Directors to elect Secretary and Treasurer.

Must be a stockholder.

No dissolution because of failure to elect.

Directors to continue in office until new elect'n

Majority may act

May call in capital stock.

Notice.

elected, and shall deliver over the subscription books to the said Directors, who may keep the same open, by a vote of the majority of stockholders, for further subscription, if the same be deemed expedient, until the entire amount of capital stock shall be subscribed; and each stockholder so subscribing, after organization of the said corporation as aforesaid, shall be bound by said election and organization until the next annual election in course, as is hereinafter provided, when he shall be entitled to vote as the original stockholders.

SEC. 4. *Be it further enacted,* That there shall be an annual meeting of the stockholders of said corporation, at such time and place as the said corporation may provide by its by-laws, for the purpose of electing Directors, and that the time of holding the first meeting of the Directors under the said first election shall be fixed by the said Directors chosen at said election, or at the annual elections to be afterwards held, shall, as soon as may be after every subsequent election, choose out of their number a President; and in case of the death, resignation or removal of the President or any Director, such vacancy or vacancies may be filled for the remainder of the year wherein they may happen by the said remaining Directors, or a majority of them; and in case of the absence of the President, the said Directors, or a majority of them, may appoint a President *pro tem.,* who shall exercise such power and functions as the by-laws of said corporation may provide.

SEC. 5. *Be it further enacted,* That the said directors, or a majority of them, shall elect, simultaneously with the President and annually, a suitable person, who shall discharge the duties of Secretary and Treasurer of said corporation, who shall be a stockholder in the same and other than a director.

SEC. 6. *Be it further enacted,* That in case it should happen that an election of directors should not be made when, pursuant to this act, it should be had, the said corporation shall not by reason thereof be dissolved, but such election shall be held at any other time, and the directors previously elected shall continue as directors until a new election shall be had; a majority of said directors of said corporation to transact all business of said corporation, and they shall have power to call in the capital stock of said Company, giving thirty days notice thereof to the said stockholders by

LAWS OF FLORIDA.

LAWS OF FLORIDA.

1859.

Forfeiture for

advertisement in some newspaper or newspapers; and in case of the non-payment of said instalment, the stockholder so failing to pay his instalment within ten days after the same becomes due, shall forfeit his share or shares and the amount before paid to the corporation.

Sec. 7. *Be it further enacted,* That the said Company shall have liberty to transport passengers, goods, wares, merchandize and all other lawful things whatsoever, and of every description, in vessels propelled by steam or otherwise, and in boats, barges, flats and lighters, and in all other conveyances by water, between such points and to such places as the said directors, or a majority of them, may designate; and the said directors, or a majority of them, may from time to time appoint such captains, commanders, agents and all other officers and employees as to them may seem proper and necessary for the interests of said corporation.

Sec. 8. *Be it further enacted,* That the directors of the said corporation, or a majority of them, shall settle and adjust the books and accounts of said corporation at least once every year, and submit a detailed statement of the affairs thereof to the stockholders at their annual meeting, and declare and pay over such dividend of the actual profits thereof as the condition of the said Company may justify; and the stockholders shall have power to adopt such by-laws for the government of said Company as they may deem proper, not inconsistent with this charter or the laws of the State of Florida.

Sec. 9. *Be it further enacted,* That the said directors, or a majority of them, shall have power to exact from the Treasurer or any other officer of said Company a bond, in such sum as they may deem proper, conditioned for the faithful performance of the duties of his said office.

Sec. 10. *Be it further enacted,* That the private property of the stockholders in said Company shall only be liable for the debts, liabilities and obligations of said Company *pro rata,* according to the amount of stock owned by each stockholder.

Sec. 11. *Be it further enacted,* That nothing in this act shall be so construed to give said Company the exclusive privilege of navigating the rivers Apalachicola, Chattahoochee and Flint.

Passed the Senate December 15, 1859. Passed the House of Representatives December 19, 1859. Approved by the Governor December 22, 1859.

CHAPTER 1,024—[No. 29.]

AN ACT declaring the Perdido river navigable.

Declared navigable.

SECTION 1. *Be it enacted by the Senate and House of Representatives of the State of Florida in General Assembly convened,* That the Perdido river shall be and is hereby declared navigable.

Penalty for obstructing navigation.

SEC. 2. *Be it further enacted,* That if any person or persons shall obstruct, or cause to be obstructed, said river, so as to prevent navigation, such person or persons shall be liable to indictment, and, on conviction thereof, shall be fined, at the discretion of the jury, in any sum not exceeding three hundred dollars.

Passed the House of Representatives December 10, 1859. Passed the Senate December 12, 1859. Approved by the Governor December 20, 1859.

CHAPTER 1,025—[No. 30.]

AN ACT to incorporate the Lake City and Suwannee Railroad Company.

Commissioners to open books of subscription.

SECTION 1. *Be it enacted by the Senate and House of Representatives of the State of Florida in General Assembly convened,* That John Eccles, John R. Herndon, Z. M. Paschall, Noble A. Hull, Edward R. Ives, William B. Ross, Calvin Peacock, James W. McQueen and Arthur J. T. Wright be and they are hereby constituted Commissioners to open books and receive subscriptions for stock in a railroad to be constructed from the city of Lake City, in the county of Columbia, to New Boston, or some other point on the Suwannee river below the head of navigation, any three of whom may open books, at such times and places as they may think proper, upon giving at least twenty days public notice thereof, and shall keep the same open until the whole capital stock is subscribed; and upon all stocks so subscribed two and a half per cent. shall be required to be paid at the time of subscription.

Notice.

Amount to be paid at time of subscription.

Capital stock may be increased, how divided.

SEC. 2. *Be it further enacted,* That the capital stock of said Company shall be two hundred thousand dollars, with the privilege of increasing it, if necessary, to three hundred thousand dollars, divided into such number of shares as a majority of the Board of Directors may determine.

SEC. 3. *Be it further enacted*, That the said Railroad shall extend from the city of Lake City to New Boston, or some other point on the navigable waters of the Suwannee river, to be determined by a majority of the Board of Directors of said Company.

Termini of road.

SEC. 4. *Be it further enacted*, That as soon as thirty thousand dollars shall have been subscribed to the capitol stock of said Company, the subscribers of said stock, their successors and assigns, shall be and they are hereby declared to be a body corporate, by the name and style of the Lake City and Suwannee Railroad Company, and by said corporate name shall be capable in law of purchasing, holding, leasing, selling and conveying real, personal and mixed property, may sue and be sued, make contracts, pass by-laws and do all lawful acts properly incident to a corporation or necessary and proper for the transaction of the business for which it is incorporated; and to have and use a common seal, and the same to alter and destroy at pleasure.

Body corporate.

Name.

May purchase and hold property.

May sue and be sued.

By-laws.
Powers.

Common seal.

SEC. 5. *Be it further enacted*, That as soon as thirty thousand dollars shall have been subscribed, the said Commissioners named in the first section of this act, or any three of them, shall call a meeting of the subscribers, at such time and place as they may appoint, and at such meeting the said subscribers, or a majority of them in value, shall elect, by ballot, seven Directors, who shall be stockholders, to manage the affairs of said Company; and at such and all future elections, each stockholder shall be entitled to one vote for each share which he or she may hold, and may vote in person or by proxy in writing; and the Directors thus chosen shall remain in office for one year, or until their successors are duly elected; and an annual election shall thereafter be held by said Company, at such time and place as the by-laws of the Company may direct or provide.

Meet'g of stockholders, when and by whom called.

Directors.

Voting, how & in what ratio.

Tenure of Directors.

SEC. 6. *Be it further enacted*, That the Board of Directors, so elected as aforesaid, shall elect one of their number to be President; and, in case any vacancy occur in the Board between two periods of general election, the remaining members of the Board shall fill such vacancy from the stockholders by the selection of a suitable person to serve until the next regular election; and if it should so happen that the day of the annual election of Directors should pass with-

Directors to choose Presid't.

Vacancies, how filled.

No dissolution for failure to elect.

1859.

out an election being effected, or any day for such election, the corporation should not thereby be dissolved or be deemed discontinued, but it shall be lawful on any other day to hold and make such election in such manner as may be prescribed by the by-laws, and, in the mean time, the President and Directors then in office shall continue to hold over until an election is effected.

Directors to continue till new election.

Board to transact business, what.

SEC. 7. *Be it further enacted*, That a majority of the Directors shall constitute a Board for the transaction of business, of whom the President shall be one, except in case of sickness or other unavoidable cause of absence, when his place may be filled *pro tempore* by the Board from one of its own members.

President pro tem.

SEC. 8. *Be it further enacted*, That the Board of Directors shall appoint all such officers, agents, engineers or servants whatsoever as they may deem necessary, and may dismiss them at pleasure, may determe the compensation of all persons in the employ of said Company, and a majority of them shall have power to call a meeting of the stockholders at any time; and said Directors are further empowered to pass all by-laws which they may deem necessary and proper for exercising all the powers vested in this Company for carrying into effect the objects of this act: *Provided*, Such by-laws shall not be contrary to the laws of this State or of the United States; and the said Directors, or a majority of them, are empowered to borrow money to carry into effect the objects of this act, to issue certificates or other evidence of such loan, and to pledge the property of said Company for the payment of the same, with interest.

Directors to appoint all officers, agents, &c.

May determine compensation.

Majority may call meeting of stockholders.

Power to pass by-laws.

Proviso.

May borrow money, issue certificates of debt and pledge property of Company.

SEC. 9. *Be it further enacted*, That the Board of Directors may call for instalments on each share of stock, in such amount, not exceeding ten per cent., at such times as they may deem necessary for the interests of the Company, giving at least sixty days notice in some newspaper published in this State of such call; and any and all stockholders failing to pay any instalment so called for, within thirty days after the time designated in such call for payment, shall forever forfeit his stock in said Company, and all instalments paid thereon, or be liable to have such balance as may be due recovered by an action of debt, at the discretion of the Company. In the event the stock be forfeited, it shall vest in and become the property of said Company and shall be disposed of as the Board of Directors shall determine.

Directors may call for instalments of stock.

Notice.

Forfeiture for non-payment.

Sec. 10. *Be it further enacted*, That certificates of stock shall be issued to the stockholders according as it is paid in, which certificates shall be transferable on the books of the Company only, and by personal entry of the stockholder, or his legally appointed attorney or agent, duly authorized in writing for that purpose.

Certificates of stock when to issue and how transferable.

Sec. 11. *Be it further enacted*, That payments of the subscription to the stock in said Railroad may be made in materials, labor and all and everything necessary for the construction of said road which the Board of Directors may, at their discretion, deem expedient to accept; and the said Board of Directors shall keep fair and regular entries of their proceedings, in a book to be provided for that purpose, which book shall be open to the inspection of the stockholders at any meeting of the Board.

Payments for subscription to the stock may be made in materials, labor, &c.

Entries of proceedings to be kept open to inspect'n of stockholders.

Sec. 12. *Be it further enacted*, That the President and Directors of said Company are hereby authorized to contract for and receive conveyances of land, stone, timber or wood which may be necessary for the construction of said railroad, and when the owner and the company cannot agree upon the price, or when the owner is an infant, non-resident, *feme covert* or *non compos mentis*, then it shall be lawful for the President and Directors of said company to apply to the Sheriff of the county in which said land or other property is situated, who shall summon a jury of five disinterested freeholders, a majority of whom shall be authorized to assess the damages and return their award to the next term of the Circuit Court for the county, which shall be entered by the Clerk as the judgment of the Court, and execution may issue thereupon for the amount of said award and costs, with the right of appeal to either party, to be tried by a special jury at that or the next ensuing term of said Circuit Court, and the decision shall vest in said company the fee simple of the land or ownership of the material in question; but the proposed work shall not be delayed on account of the proceedings had as aforesaid.

Directors may receive conveyances of land, materials, &c.

Proceedings when no agreement with own'r upon the price, or owner be an infant or non compos mentis.

Sec. 13. *Be it further enacted*, That the jurors summoned as aforesaid, before proceeding to the discharge of the duties herein required, shall take an oath or affirmation, administered by the Sheriff, that they will well and truly inquire into, and to the best of their judgment assess the damages accruing to the owner or owners of such lands or

Oath of jury.

materials, or lands and materials, by means of the proposed construction.

SEC. 14. *Be it further enacted,* That if any person shall wilfully injure or obstruct in any degree said road, he shall forfeit and pay to the President and Directors of said company four times the amount of all damages they may sustain in consequence thereof, to be sued for and recovered in the manner now provided by law for individuals in like cases; and on complaint to any Justice of the Peace within whose jurisdiction such offence shall be committed, it shall be the duty of such Justice of the Peace to bind the person or persons so offending, with sufficient security for his or their good behavior, for one year, and such offender shall also be subjected to indictment, and shall be sentenced, at the discretion of the Court, to be imprisoned not less than three nor more than six months.

Forfeiture for injury or obstruction to road

Offender to be bound for good behavior to Magistrate.

Indictment and penalty against.

SEC. 15. *Be it further enacted,* That in the construction of said railroad, the President and Directors of said Company shall in no manner obstruct any public road now established, but shall provide convenient passages to travel over said road, and any public or private road may at any time be constructed across said Railroad: *Provided,* Such public or private road shall not at all obstruct or incommode the free use of said Railroad.

Company not to obstruct public road.

Public or private road may cross railroad.

Proviso.

SEC. 16. *Be it further enacted,* That after the completion of said road, or any part thereof, the said President and Directors may lay and collect tolls from all persons, property, merchandize and other commodities transported thereon: *Provided,* The net profits on said road shall not exceed twenty-five per cent. per annum upon the capital stock.

President and Directors may lay and collect tolls.

Proviso.

SEC. 17. *Be it further enacted,* That the said Railroad and its appurtenances, and all property herewith connected, shall not be taxed higher than one-half of one per cent. upon its annual net income.

Limit of taxation on railroad.

SEC. 18. *Be it further enacted,* That the said Railroad be and it is hereby declared a proper improvement to be aided by the Internal Improvement Fund, as expressed in section 29, in this State, under act of the General Assembly entitled an act to provide for and encourage a liberal system of Internal Improvements in this State, approved 6th January, 1855, and shall be entitled to and receive the alternate sections of State land for six miles on each side of said road as

Grant of alternate sections of land to Co.

soon as said road is completed, in the same manner as if said road had extended beyond thirty miles: *Provided,* Said Company shall in all respects comply with the requirements of said Internal Improvement act and the laws amendatory thereto. **Proviso.**

SEC. 19. *Be it further enacted,* That the Company hereby incorporated shall commence the building of their road within three years and complete the same within five years from the passage of this act. **Road to be commenced and be completed**

Passed the Senate December 12, 1859. Passed the House of Representatives December 20, 1859. Approved by the Governor December 22, 1859.

CHAPTER 1,026—[No. 31.]

AN ACT more fully defining the Duties of Tax-Assessors and Collectors for the City of Pensacola.

SECTION 1. *Be it enacted by the Senate and House of Representatives of the State of Florida in General Assembly convened,* That hereafter when any tax imposed under the by-laws or ordinances of the City of Pensacola upon real or personal property, shall be unpaid for the space of twenty days after the same shall have been due, the tax-collector of said city shall, by advertisement for the space of thirty days in some newspaper published in said city, give notice to the owner of the property on which the said tax shall have been assessed, that the said city will apply to the next term of the Circuit Court of Escambia County where the tax shall exceed fifty dollars, or to a justice of the Peace of said city on some day occurring after thirty days from the first publication of said advertisement, when the amount of tax shall not exceed fifty dollars, for a judgment in behalf of said city for said tax against said property, and the said advertisement shall describe the property on which the said tax shall be due, and state the amount of the tax, but shall not designate the owner of the said property; and on the first day of the term of said Court occurring after said advertisement, or on the day mentioned in said advertisement, for the application to a Justice of the Peace, the said Tax-Collector shall present to said Court or Justice of the Peace a petition, under oath, in behalf of said city, stating the **Notice to be given by Tax Collector.**

Description of property and amount of tax.

Petition to be presented to Circuit Co'rt or Justice of the Peace.

7

amount of tax, the non-payment thereof and describing the property on which the same was assessed, and within three days after the filing of the said petition the owner of the said property, or his attorney, may file the following objections to said petition, but no other, to wit: That the said tax is unauthorized by law, or that the same, together with all costs, if any, has been paid; and thereupon the said Court

or Justice of the Peace shall proceed to adjudge the matter, and, if the objection shall be sustained, the petition shall be dismissed and a judgment for costs shall be rendered against said city; but if said objection shall be overruled, or if no objection shall be filed within three days after presentation of said petition, the said Court or Justice of the Peace shall,

if satisfied that the advertisement aforesaid has been made, render judgment against the said property for the amount of said tax, with interest and costs, in which shall be included the expense of the adverti-ement aforesaid, upon

which judgment an execution shall issue and be satisfied by the sale of so much of said property as may be necessary for that purpose.

SEC. 2. *Be it further enacted.* That all proceedings under the execution issued as aforesaid shall be governed by the same rules and regulations, except when herein otherwise provided, as are prescribed by law in the case of other executions: and a sale and deed made and executed by the

Sheriff or Constable, under such execution, shall be as effectual to divest the title of the owner of the property as though the same had been executed by said owner: *Provided, however.* That the said owner, or his or her agent,

shall be entitled to redeem the said property by depositing with the Treasurer of said city the amount paid by the purchaser, and fifty per cent. thereon, within one year after said sale, and notifying said purchaser of said deposit, and the

certificate of the said Treasurer that said deposit has been made shall render the deed of the said Sheriff or Constable to said purchaser null and void.

SEC. 3. *Be it further enacted,* That at the sale under execution, hereinbefore provided for, the person who shall offer to satisfy the same for a smaller quantity or portion of the property than any other person present shall be deemed the

highest bidder, and no bid shall be received unless it be for a specific portion of the property, and, in the case of real estate, unless the bidder shall designate the portion proposed to be taken by metes and bounds.

Sec. 4. *Be it further enacted*, That the tax imposed on any lot or parcel of land within the corporate limits of said city, held in common or in parcenary, shall be charged on the whole lot or parcel, and any specific portion thereof may be sold to satisfy said execution, and each sale shall work a severance of the tenantry in common or parcenary as to the specific portion sold, and the purchaser thereof shall hold the same in severalty. *Tax on land held in common or in parcenary, charged on the whole.* *Tax sale to work severance.* *Purchaser to hold in severalty*

Sec. 5. *Be it further enacted*, That the Mayor of the said city shall be and he is hereby authorized to hear and determine all cases involving a breach of the ordinance of said city, and to impose and enforce such punishment, by fine or imprisonment, as the said ordinances may authorize. *Mayor of city authorized to determine violations of ordinances. To impose and enforce punishments.]*

Sec. 6. *Be it further enacted*, That all fines, forfeitures, penalties and taxes, not herein otherwise provided for, shall be enforced and collected by the seizure or distress and sale of real or personal property, in the manner prescribed by the ordinances or by-laws of said city. *Fines, forfeitures, &c., how enforced & collected.*

Sec. 7. *Be it further enacted*, That taxes heretofore imposed and assessed by said city, which remain unpaid, shall be collected in the mode prescribed by this act. *Taxes heretofore imposed, how collected.*

Sec. 8. *Be it further enacted*, That no alderman or other officer of the said city, nor any director, officer or agent of any Railroad Company, or other incorporated association, in any way interested in the revenue of said city, nor any person not a resident or freeholder therein, shall be eligible to the office of appraiser or assessor for taxes in said city. *Who eligible to office of appraiser or Tax Assessor.*

Sec. 9. *Be it further enacted*, That the Tax-Assessors for the said city of Pensacola shall, before entering upon the duties of their office, give bond and take oath in the same manner and be subject to the same penalties as is now provided by law for assessors for State and county purposes, and the said oath shall be in the following form: I, A B, do solemnly swear (or affirm) that I will make all assessments fairly and impartially, according to the best of my judgment, and at what I believe to be the actual and true value of property within the corporate limits of this city at the present time, &c. *Bond and oath of Tax Assessor.*

Sec. 10. *Be it further enacted*, That this act shall not be in force until the Mayor and Board of Aldermen of said *When Act to be in force.*

Repeal.

city shall have signified their assent thereto by entering such assent on the journal of their proceedings.

SEC. 11. *Be it further enacted,* That all acts and parts of acts conflicting with the true intent and meaning of this act be and the same are hereby repealed.

Passed the Senate December 10, 1859. Passsd the House of Representatives December 15, 1859. Approved by the Governor December 21, 1859.

CHAPTER 1,027—[No. 32.]

AN ACT to amend an act entitled an act to amend an act entitled an act to incorporate the town of Quincy, approved February 12th, 1837, approved January 13th, 1859.

SECTION 1. *Be it enacted by the Senate and House of Representatives of the State of Florida in General Assembly convened,* That section four of an act entitled an act to incorporate the town of Quincy, approved February 12th, 1837, be and the same is hereby declared to be in full force as though the act entitled an act to amend an act entitled an act to incorporate the town of Quincy, approved February 12th, 1837, approved January 13th, 1859, had not been passed.

Re-enactment of 4th section of Act of 1837.

SEC. 2. *Be it further enacted,* That section two of an act to which this is an amendment be so amended as to read as follows:

What persons & property subjected to corporate authority.

That all persons and private property comprised and being within the above-described limits shall be subject to the same corporate authority and to the same ordinances, laws and regulations of the Town Council of the said town corporation as are the persons and private property now within the present limits of said corporation.

SEC. 3. *Be it further enacted,* That section three of an act to which this is an amendment be so amended as to read as follows:

Proceedings on refusal of persons to grant right of way for streets or failure to agree with town authorities as to damages.

That if any person or persons owning or controlling the lands over which the corporate limits of said town have been extended by this act shall refuse to give the right of way to said town for the extension of streets, as hereinbefore provided for, and said person or persons shall fail to agree with the authorities of said town as to the damages sustained, or that may be sustained by said person or persons in consequence of the extension of said streets through his, her or their lands, then, in that case, it shall be the duty of the Intendant and Town Council to appoint three discreet and disinterested freeholders of said town or county to act as Commissioners, whose duty it shall be, after being duly sworn by the Intendant, or other officer authorized to ad- Oath and duty of minister oaths, faithfully and impartially to discharge the Commissioners. duties of such Commissioners, to view the premises and assess damages to the person or persons through whose lands said streets may be extended; and it shall also be the duty of said Commissioners to assess the benefits that may accrue to the owner or owners of the land through which said street or streets are to be opened and extended: *Provided, how-* Proviso. *ever*, That in no case shall the Commissioners assess benefits to a greater amount than the damages, and the benefits so assessed shall be deducted from the damages sustained, and Damages and the balance, if any remain, shall be paid by the town of costs to be paid. Quincy to the person or persons damaged, together with all costs of the proceeding.

SEC. 4. *Be it further enacted*, That all laws and parts Repeal. of laws conflicting with this act be and the same are hereby repealed.

Passed the House of Representatives December 14, 1859. Passed the Senate December 22, 1859. Approved by the Governor December 22, 1859.

CHAPTER 1,028—[No. 33.]

AN ACT to correct an error in the printed act entitled an act to incorporate the city of Lake City.

SECTION 1. *Be it enacted by the Senate and House of Representatives of the State of Florida in General As- sembly convened*, That the corporate limits of the city of Corporate limits. Lake City be and they are hereby declared to be compre- hended within the following bounds: That is to say, half a mile South, East and West, and three-quarters of a mile North of the Court House of Columbia county, in every direction therefrom.

SEC. 2. *Be it further enacted*, That all laws and parts of Repeal.

laws conflicting with the true intent and meaning of this act be and the same are hereby repealed.

Passed the Senate December 3, 1859. Passed the House of Representatives December 7, 1859. Approved by the Governor December 19, 1859.

CHAPTER 1,029—[No. 34.]

AN ACT to amend an act amending the Charter of the City of Pensacola, for the purpose of extending the powers of the city to aid in the construction of the Alabama and Florida Railroad in Florida, approved December 21st, 1858.

Be it enacted by the Senate and House of Representatives of the State of Florida in General Assembly convened, That the second section of said act be so amended as to authorize the city of Pensacola to endorse or guarantee the bonds of the Alabama and Florida Railroad Company to the extent of one hundred and thirty thousand dollars, said endorsement or guarantee to be made in such manner and under such restrictions as the Mayor and Board of Aldermen shall prescribe.

City authorized to guarantee bonds.

Limitation.

How to be made.

Passed the Senate December 19, 1859. Passed the House of Representatives December 22, 1859. Approved December 22, 1859.

CHAPTER 1,030—[No. 35.]

AN ACT to amend an act entitled an act to incorporate the city of Atseena Otie.

SECTION 1. *Be it enacted by the Senate and House of Representatives of the State of Florida in General Assembly convened,* That the corporate limits of the city of Atseena Otie be so extended as to embrace the ship channel from Atseena Otie to the Island known as Sea Horse Key, together with all the anchorage ground between those two points.

Extension of corporate limits.

SEC. 2. *Be it further enacted,* That if any master of any vessel shall violate any of the quarantine regulations established or to be established by the City Council of Atseena Otie, or knowingly permit any of his officers, or crew, or

Master of vessel violating or permitting violation of quarantine regulations subject to forfeiture.

passengers on board his said vessel, to violate such ordinances, such master shall forfeit the penalty already prescribed in the ordinances of said city, or which may hereafter be prescribed, and be subject to indictment for such offence in any Court having competent jurisdiction, and, on conviction, shall be fined by the Court in a sum not exceeding one hundred dollars.

And indictment.

Penalty.

SEC. 3. *Be it further enacted,* That the City Council of Atseena Otie shall have power to impose such tax as they may deem just and proper on all persons exhibiting any shows, circus performances or other exhibitions for public amusements, and to prohibit the sale of spiritous liquors in quantities less than one barrel, except under license, to be granted to the vendors thereof by the City Council, the cost of which license shall be at the discretion of the City Council; and for each and every violation of the provisions of any ordinance which may be enacted in pursuance of the provisions of this act, the said City Council shall have power to impose such penalty and forfeiture as they may deem proper: *Provided,* Such penalty or forfeiture shall not exceed fifty dollars for each offence.

Power of City Council to tax shows, &c.

To prohibit sale of liquor without license.

License tax.

To impose penalty, &c., for violations of ordinances.

Limitation.

SEC. 4. *Be it further enacted,* That the provisions of this act shall not be so construed as to effect in any manner the commerce and navigation of the sea-port of Cedar Keys or Atseena Otie, except only for the purpose of a proper police regulation of the said port.

Act not to affect commerce and navigation.

Passed the House of Representatives December 14, 1859. Passed the Senate December 20, 1859. Approved December 22, 1859.

CHAPTER 1,031.—[No. 36.]

AN ACT to authorize the Mayor and Aldermen of the City of Pensacola to elect a Public Weigher of Cotton.

SECTION 1. *Be it enacted by the Senate and House of Representatives of the State of Florida in General Assembly convened.* That there shall be elected by the Mayor and Aldermen of the City of Pensacola on the first Monday of February of each and every year, one Public Weigher of Cotton, who shall weigh all cotton brought to market in the usual bales or packages, with his own Scales or Balan-

Mayor and Aldermen may elect weigher.

When.]

Duty of

Term of office of.

How and for what removed.

Vacancy, how filled.

ces. He shall hold his office for the term of one year and until his successor is elected and qualified, subject to removal at any time by a majority of Aldermen, for gross and palpable misconduct. When vacancy may occur by death, resignation or removal, the Mayor may appoint until the next regular meeting of the Board of Aldermen.

Oath of weigher.

To be in readiness at all times

May employ assistant.
Oath of.
Responsible for acts of.

Certificate to be given.

SEC. 2. *Be it further enacted,* That the person so elected, before entering upon the duties of his office, shall take an oath to be administered by a Justice of the Peace, or other person authorized to administer oaths, faithfully and impartially to execute the duties of his office and make true returns; he shall be in readiness at all times during business hours to discharge said duty; he shall have power to appoint and employ an assistant, who shall also be sworn to perform his duty, and for whose acts the principal shall be responsible. He shall certify the weight in detail, and at the request of the seller or purchaser, the merchantable condition of the Cotton weighed by him.

Liability and penalty for malfeasance & fraud

SEC. 3. *Be it further enacted,* That he shall be liable in any Court of competent jurisdiction for malfeasance in office and fraud, and on conviction, shall be removed from office and shall be liable to damages at the suit of the party aggrieved.

To keep scales and weights.

To mark bales.

SEC. 4. *Be it further enacted,* That he shall keep accurate and well adjusted Scales or Balances and accurate weights, and shall mark with ink, and in legible characters on each bale, the weight thereof, and when required, the initials of his name and office.

Allowances to. Who to designate.

Lieu therefor.

SEC. 5. *Be it further enacted,* That he shall be allowed for each bale weighed, marked and certified by him any sum the said Mayor and Aldermen may designate, not to exceed twenty-five cents per bale; and he shall not be obliged to deliver cotton so weighed and marked until the said charge shall be paid and satisfied.

When act to go in force.

SEC. 6. *Be it further enacted,* That that this act shall be in force from and after February next.

Passed the House of Representatives December 9, 1859. Passed the Senate December 12, 1859. Approved by the Governor December 20, 1859.

CHAPTER 1,032—[No. 37.]

AN ACT to secure the right of way to the St. John's and Indian River Canal, and for other purposes.

SECTION 1. *Be it enacted by the Senate and House of Representatives of the State of Florida in General Assembly convened*, That the Commissioners of the St. Johns and Indian River Canal be, and they are hereby authorized to construct said Canal upon the public lands of the State of Florida, whether the same be Internal Improvement, Swamp and Overflowed, School, Seminary or other lands, so far as the line of said Canal shall be made to pass through the same, and the said Commissioners shall have the privilege of using the timber, earth, stone, or other material on said lands, on each side of said Canal in the construction and repair thereof.

Grant of right of way over State lands.

Privilege to use timber, &c.

SEC. 2. *Be it further enacted*, That in constructing the said Canal, it shall and may be lawful for the said Canal Commissioners by its or their proper agents or servants to enter upon and take possession of any land belonging to individuals which may be necessary for the way, and for the completion of the work incident to said Canal, and also such timber, stone, or other materials as may be necessary for the construction and keeping in repair the same; *Provided*, that nothing belonging to individuals shall be taken without adequate compensation, to be determined in the manner hereinafter provided for.

Right to enter upon land of indiv'duals granted, and to use timber, stone,&c therefrom.

Compensation to be paid therefor.

SEC. 3. *Be it further enacted*, That whenever it shall become necessary for the said Commissioners to take possession of, and appropriate, or use any land, timber, stone, or other material owned by private individuals for the route or site of the said Canal, or for constructing and keeping in repair the same, or any part thereof, and the parties do not agree on the value and sale of the land, timber, stone, or other materials as may be so taken or appropriated, it shall and may be lawful for the said Canal Commissioners, or their proper agent or agents on giving twenty day's notice at least, in writing, to the party owning the same, or to his, her, or their agent, if the owner is known, or if the owner is not known, or the lands are in dispute between two or more claimants, then by thirty day's publication in some newspaper published ·

Proceedings to assess value of land, timber, &c. when owner and Commissioners cannot agree on same.

8

at the Town of Jacksonville, Florida, that application will be made to the Judge of the Probate Court of the County of Volusia, Florida, for a writ of *ad quod damnum*, which shall be granted, and directed to the Sheriff of the County of Volusia, to summon five disinterested persons, householders of lawful age, to meet and value the said land, stone, timber, or other materials as the case may be, on oath, to be administered by any Justice of the Peace, whose duty it shall be to attend in person said inquest, and receive their report, and if from any cause, a Justice of the Peace does not attend said inquest, then the sheriff aforesaid shall and may administer the oath and receive the report ; the amount thus fixed upon by said valuation the said Justice of the Peace or Sheriff shall receive from the said Commissioners or their proper agent, and pay the same over to the person or persons so entitled to receive it, and to take an acquittal or refusal for the same, and on tender of the sum awarded to the party entitled to receive the same, or to his, her, or their agent or attorney, it shall be lawful for said Commissioners to enter upon and take possession of and use any such lands, stone, timber and other materials ; but all costs and expenses incurred by said writ of *ad quod damnum* and inquest shall be paid by the said Canal Commissioners ; *Provided*, That the appraisers shall not be allowed more than one dollar each per day whilst engaged in such duties and the Justice of the Peace and Sheriff such fees as are usual in similar cases.

Forfeiture for injury or obstruction to Canal or property of same.

Sec. 4. *Be it further enacted*, That in case any person shall wilfully injure or obstruct in any degree the said Canal, or any part thereof, or wilfully injure any property, real or personal belonging to the same, he shall forfeit and pay to the said Canal Commissioners three times the amount of all damages they may sustain in consequence thereof, to be sued for and recovered in the same manner as provided by law for individuals in like cases, and on complaint to any magistrate within whose jurisdiction such offence shall be committed, it shall be the duty of such magistrate to bind the person or persons so offending, with sufficient security, for his or their good behavior for a period of not less than one year, and such offenders shall also be subjected to indictment, and shall be sentenced to imprisonment at the discretion of the Court, and to remain committed until all costs are paid.

Party offending to be bound over

Indictment therefor and punishment.

Passed the House of Representatives December 16, 1859.   Passed the Senate December 20, 1859.   Approved by the Governor December 22, 1859.

CHAPTER 1,033—[No. 38.]

AN ACT to grant alternate sections of Swamp and Overflowed Lands to the
Perdido Railroad Company.

SECTION 1. *Be it enacted by the Senate and House of
Representatives of the State of Florida in General Assem-*
bly convened, That, from and after the passage of this act, Trustees of Int.
the Board of Internal Improvements may have the power Imp. Fund authorized to grant
to grant to the Perdido Railroad Company such alternate land to.
sections of swamp and overflowed lands now lying and being in Escambia county as they may deem necessary and
proper to be granted, to aid in the construction of said road
and for clearing out the Perdido river and draining the lands
adjacent thereto.

Passed the House of Representatives December 21, 1859.   Passed the Senate December 22, 1859.   Approved by the Governor December 22, 1859.

CHAPTER 1,034—[No. 39.]

AN ACT to change the time of holding the Circuit Court in the counties of
Hamilton and Taylor, in the Middle Judicial Circuit of Florida.

SECTION 1. *Be it enacted by the Senate and House of
Representatives of the State of Florida in General Assem-*
bly convened, That the spring term of the Circuit Court shall Spring Terms
be held in the county of Hamilton on the third Monday in in Hamilton.
April, and the fall term of said Court in said county on the Fall Term.
third Monday in November in each year.

SEC. 2. *Be it further enacted,* That the spring term of Spring Term in
the Circuit Court shall be held in the county of Taylor on Taylor.
the fourth Monday in April, and the fall term of said Court Fall Term.
in said county on the fourth Monday in November in each
year.

SEC. 3. *Be it further enacted,* That this act shall take When act to
effect and be in force from and after the first day of Janu- take effect.
ary, 1860.

SEC. 4. *Be it further enacted,* That all acts coming in Repeal.
conflict with this be and the same are hereby repealed.

Passed the House of Representatives December 6th, 1859.   Passed the Senate December 9, 1859.   Approved by the Governor December 19, 1859.

CHAPTER 1,035—[No. 40.]

AN ACT to amend an act to provide for the recording of Marks and Brands of Cattle shipped from the counties of Manatee and Hillsborough, passed at the ninth General Assembly, approved by the Governor January 13th, 1859.

Duty of person intending to drive or ship cattle.

SECTION 1. *Be it enacted by the Senate and House of Representatives of the State of Florida in General Assembly convened*, That the second section of the act to which this is an amendment be and it is hereby amended, that it shall be the duty of any person or persons who shall intend to drive or ship Beef Cattle out of the limits and range of Manatee county, with the intention of selling or otherwise disposing of the same, to notify the inspector and recorder of marks and brands of the said county, in writing or other responsible manner, stating the time and place when the said inspector or recorder shall attend to inspect and record the marks and brands of said cattle; and it shall be the duty of the said inspector and recorder to attend at the time and place designated, and there examine and truly record the marks and brands of the said cattle to the best of his knowledge and ability.

Notice to inspector and recorder to be given.

Duty [of inspector and recorder

Inspector and recorder to be appointed by County Commissioners.

SEC. 2. *Be it further enacted*, That the inspector and recorder of marks and brands specified in this act and the act to which this is an amendment shall be appointed by the Board of County Commissioners of the county of Manatee, and such inspector shall give bond and security for the faithful performance of his duties in such sum as the said Board of County Commissioners shall determine; and the said bond shall be given to the Judge of Probate and his successors in office, and shall be approved by the Judge of Probate and Board of County Commissioners; and said inspector shall file said bond and make oath faithfully to perform his duty before entering upon the duties of his office; and said inspector shall return the said inspection and record of marks and brands by him taken to the Circuit Clerk of Manatee county, to be recorded according to law, and said return shall be made within thirty days.

To give bond.

Oath.

Return of inspection and record to whom and when to be made and where recorded.

May appoint deputies.

SEC. 3. *Be it further enacted*, That said inspector be and he is hereby authorized to appoint deputies, who shall be duly qualified, and he shall be responsible for their acts; and said inspector shall pay the Clerk's fees for recording

Shall pay fees for recording.

the marks and brands, and the inspector shall furnish the person or persons for whom the inspection is made with a certificate of inspection, which certificate shall be in evidence in all Courts in this State. *Certificate of Inspection.*

Sec. 4. *Be it further enacted,* That all laws or parts of laws conflicting with the true intent and meaning of this act be and the same are hereby repealed. *Repeal.*

Passed the House of Representatives December 14, 1859. Passed the Senate December 20, 1859. Approved by the Governor December 22, 1859.

Chapter 1,036.—[No. 41.]

AN ACT to amend an act entitled an act to organize the county of Volusia, approved Jan. 29th, 1854.

Section 1. *Be it enacted by the Senate and House of Representatives of the State of Florida in General Assembly convened,* That the 11th section of the said act to organize the county of Volusia be, and the same is hereby construed to refer to all monies of the county of Orange then in the control of the Treasurer, Sheriff, or [other] officer of said county ; or at that time due for taxes or otherwise to the said county of Orange previous to its division, or which have been since collected. *Construction of 11 section of act of 1854.*

Sec. 2. *Be it further enacted,* That all the monies then in the control of the Treasurer or other officer of said county of Orange at the time of the approval of said act, or then due the said county in any manner, or which may have been since collected or recovered from amounts then due, be paid into the hands of the Judge of the Eastern Circuit, to be by him equitably divided between the counties of Orange and Volusia. *Monies under control of officers of Orange Co. to be divided by Judge of Eastern Circuit between Orange & Volusia Cos.*

Sec. 3. *Be it further enacted,* That upon the failure or refusal of the Treasurer or other officer of said county, or either of them, to pay over the monies as above provided to the Judge of the Circuit Court upon demand, such proceedings may be had against such officers so failing to pay over as is now provided by law against defaulting Sheriffs or other county officers. *Proceedings against Treasurer or other officer for failure to pay over money to Judge.*

Passed the Senate December 7, 1859. Passed the House of Representatives December 10, 1859. Approved by the Governor December 19, 1859.

CHAPTER 1,037—[No. 42.]

AN ACT for filling Offices in the County of Brevard.

SECTION 1. *Be it enacted by the Senate and House of Representatives of the State of Florida in General Assembly convened,* That the Governor of the State of Florida is authorized to appoint and commission any competent persons in the county of Brevard to fill any and all vacancies which now or may hereafter exist in said county; and the person so appointed and commissioned shall hold office until said office for which said appointment shall be made shall be filled by election and qualification; and the Governor shall have the power to remove any one from office whom he may appoint whenever in his judgment the public good requires such removal.

SEC. 2. *Be it further enacted,* That the Sheriff of said County shall be ex-officio Tax Assessor and Collector of said county.

Governor authorized to fill all vacancies

Term of office.

Governor may remove person appointed.

Sheriff ex-officio Tax Assessor & Collector.

Passed the House of Representatives December 17, 1859. Passed the Senate December 22, 1859. Approved by the Governor December 22, 1859.

CHAPTER 1,038—[No. 43.]

AN ACT to make the Road Laws of Duval County now in force applicable to Manatee.

SECTION 1. *Be it enacted by the Senate and House of Representatives of the State of Florida in General Assembly convened,* That the Road Laws of Duval County now in force in said County be and they are hereby made applicable to Manatee county from and after the passage of this act.

Road Law of Duval applicable to Manatee.

Passed the House of Representatives December 16, 1859. Passed the Senate December 22, 1859. Approved by the Governor December 22, 1859.

CHAPTER 1,039—[No. 44.]

AN ACT to amend an act entitled an act to divide the county of Duval and organize a new county to be called Clay county, approved by the Governor December 31, 1858.

SECTION 1. *Be it enacted by the Senate and House of Representatives of the State of Florida in General Assembly convened,* That, from and after the passage of this act, the boundary lines of Clay county shall be as follows, to wit: Beginning at the West margin of the channel of the St. Johns river, at the dividing line between towhship (3) three and (4) four, South, of range (26) twenty-six, East; thence West by said line to the range line dividing ranges (22) twenty-two and (23) twenty-three, East; thence South, along said range line, to its intersection with the Bellamy or Federal road leading from St. Augustine to Tallahassee; thence East, along the North margin of said road to its intersection with the St. Johns river; thence due East to the West margin of the channel of said river; thence down said West margin North to the place of beginning. **Boundary line of Clay county.**

SEC. 2. *Be it further enacted,* That, from and after the passage of this act, the county site of the county of Clay shall be and the same is hereafter known and designated as Webster. **County site.**

SEC. 3. *Be it further enacted,* That all that part of the county of Clay which is South of the Northern margin of the Bellamy or Federal road aforesaid shall be embraced in and constitute a part of the county of Putnam. **Part of Clay annexed to Putnam county.**

Passed the House of Representatives December 12, 1859. Passed the Senate December 22d, 1859. Approved by the Governor December 22d, 1859.

CHAPTER 1,040—[No. 45.]

AN ACT in reference to Common Schools in the county of Walton.

SECTION 1. *Be it enacted by the Senate and House of Representatives of the State of Florida in General Assembly convened,* That the Board of County Commissioners of Walton county shall have authority to receive the amounts appropriated from the Common School Fund of the State to **County Commissioners authorized to receive and loan out Common Sch'l Fund.**

Walton county for Common Schools and loan the same out, with proper security to be taken therefor, at the highest rate of interest which can be legally obtained for such loan, whenever, in the judgment of said Board, it may be deemed best for the educational interest of said county.

Passed the House of Representatives December 17, 1859. Passed the Senate December 20, 1859. Approved by the Governor December 22, 1859.

CHAPTER 1,041—[No. 46.]

AN ACT relative to the Office of Circuit Court Clerk in the County of Washington.

Clerk's office, where to be kept

SECTION 1. *Be it enacted by the Senate and House of Representatives of the State of Florida in General Assembly convened*, That from and after the passage of this act it shall not be lawful for the Clerk of the Circuit Court in and for the county of Washington to hold or keep office at any other place than the county site of said County, or in the distance of five miles thereof.

Repeal.

SEC. 2. *Be it further enacted*, That all acts or parts of acts conflicting in any manner with the true intent and meaning of this act be and the same are hereby repealed.

Passed the Senate December 12, 1859. Passsd the House of Representatives December 15, 1859. Approved by the Governor December 22, 1859.

CHAPTER 1,042—[No. 47.]

AN ACT authorizing a Bridge Tax in Walton county.

County Commissioners authorized to levy a bridge tax.

SECTION 1. *Be it enacted by the Senate and House of Representatives of the State of Florida in General Assembly convened*, That the Board of County Commissioners of Walton county shall, in addition to the tax now authorized by law to be levied for county purposes, levy a bridge tax not exceeding the rate of twenty-five per centum on the State tax in each and every year, to be assessed and collected in the same manner and under the same rules and regulations as the taxes for county purposes.

Limitation.

How collected.

SEC. 2. *Be it further enacted*, That the taxes so levied and collected shall be appropriated by the Board of County Commissioners for the building and repairing of bridges over the streams crossing the public roads of said county which are over twenty feet in distance from bank to bank, whenever and wherever they may deem it necessary. *Tax how to be appropriated.*

SEC. 3. *Be it further enacted*, That the provisions of this act shall apply to Walton county only.

Passed the Senate December 9, 1859. Passed the House of Representatives December 12, 1859. Approved December 19, 1859.

CHAPTER 1,043—[No. 48.]

AN ACT to create and regulate Pilotage at the Port of Bay Port in the County of Hernando.

SECTION 1. *Be it enacted by the Senate and House of Representatives of the State of Florida in General Assembly convened*, That the Port Wardens of the Port of Bay Port, Hernando County, be, and they are hereby authorized to appoint one or more persons to act as pilots for the bar and harbor of Bay Port, and to establish the rates and rules of pilotage for the same, and to furnish the pilots with a certified copy of the same. *Port Wardens authorized to appoint pilot & establish rates and rules of pilotage.*

SEC. 2. *Be it further enacted*, That if any person who has not been regularly appointed as above directed, shall act as pilot to any vessel, and actually pilot it into the harbor of Bay Port, and receive compensation for the same, shall be fined in a sum not exceeding thirty dollars for each and every offence, recoverable before any Justice of the Peace for the County of Hernando; one-half to the informant, the balance to revert into the county treasury for county purposes. *Fine for acting as pilots without appointment. How recovered. To whom paid.*

SEC. 3. *Be it further enacted*, That from and after the passage of this act, it shall be lawful for the several pilots of the Port of Bay Port to make such charges for pilotage as are allowed in the act governing the rates of pilotage at the port of Cedar Keys; and the pilotage at the port of Bay Port shall be governed in all respects where the same can be *Pilots, what allowed to charge and by what law to be governed.*

1859.

made applicable by the act governing Pilotage at the Port of Cedar Key.

Passed the House of Representatives December 12, 1859. Passed the Senate December 17, 1859. Approved by the Governor December 20, 1859.

CHAPTER 1,044—[No. 49.]

AN ACT amending the Pilot Laws for the Bay and Harbor of the City of Pensacola.

SECTION 1. *Be it enacted by the Senate and House of Representatives of the State of Florida in General Assembly convened,* That the 13th section of an act for the regulation of Pilots and Pilotage for the Bay and Harbor of Pensacola, approved January the 13th, 1855, be so amended as to authorize a combination or copartnership of Pilots to exist in the following manner, to wit: when there are as many four and not exceeding six lawful Pilots, having full branches to take vessels in or out of said Bay and Harbor of Pensacola, then a combination or co-partnership of not exceeding three Pilots may exist; and when there shall be seven and not exceeding eight lawful Pilots for said Bay and Harbor, then a combination or co-partnership of not exceeding four Pilots may exist: *Provided, however,* That no Pilot authorized to take vessels in or out of the Bay and Harbor of Pensacola, shall be directly or indirectly interested in the earnings of any Pilot Boat or Boats, combination or co-partnership of Pilots for said Bay and Harbor other than the one he belongs to as owner or co-partner.

Combinations and co-partnership between pilots authorized

Manner of.

Proviso.

SEC. 2. *Be it further enacted,* That whenever any master of any vessel coming into the Bay or Harbor of Pensacola without a Pilot, and not having been spoken by any Pilot coming in, shall be liable to the same Pilotage going out as he would have been had he been spoken.

Vessels coming in without pilot, liable to pilotage going out.

SEC. 3. *Be it further enacted,* That no vessel coming into the Bay and Harbor of Pensacola shall be exempt from paying pilotage, except vessels drawing eight feet or less than eight feet of water, owned or belonging within said Bay or Harbor of Pensacola or the State of Florida.

What vessels exempt from pilotage.

SEC. 4. *Be it further enacted,* That each Pilot for the

Copy of pilot

Bay and Harbor of Pensacola be furnished with a copy of the Pilot Laws.

SEC. 5. *Be it further enacted*, That all laws and parts of laws conflicting with the true intent and meaning of this act be and the same are hereby repealed.

Passed the Senate December 8, 1859. Passed the House of Representatives December 17, 1859. Approved by the Governor December 22, 1859.

Repeal.

CHAPTER 1,045—[No. 50.]

AN ACT repealing certain acts passed in relation to the County Officers of Calhoun County.

SECTION 1. *Be it enacted by the Senate and House of Representatives of the State of Florida in General Assembly convened*, That from and after the first day of February next, it shall be the duty of the Judge of Probate, Clerk of the Circuit Court and Sheriff of Calhoun county, and of each of them, to keep their respective offices, and all the papers belonging thereto, at the Court House of said county, or within one-half mile of said Court House.

SEC. 2. *Be it further enacted*, That before this act shall be in force, it shall be submitted to the qualified voters of said county of Calhoun, at their next election of Judge of Probate for said county, for approval or disapproval, at which said election the voters shall endorse on their ballots the words "approval" or "disapproval," and if a majority of the votes so cast at said election be for "approval," then this act shall be in force; if "disapproval," then the said law shall not be in force.

SEC. 3. *Be it further enacted*, That it shall be the duty of the Judge of Probate in the county of Calhoun, at the next election after the passage of this act for Judge of Probate in said county, to give notice of this act; and the canvassers of said election shall, and it is hereby made their duty, when they meet to canvass the election returns for said office of Judge of Probate, to canvass the votes for "approval" or "disapproval," and to make return thereof as in other cases of election.

Offices of Judge of Probate, Cl'k and Sheriff, where to be kept

Act to be submitted to voters for approval or disapproval.

Judge of Probate to give notice of act.

Duty of canvassers.

SEC. 4. *Be it further enacted*, That all laws conflicting with this act be and the same are hereby repealed.

Passed the House of Representatives December 7, 1859. Passed the Senate December 19, 1859. Approved by the Governor December 22, 1859.

CHAPTER 1,046—[No. 51.]

AN ACT to alter and define the line between Gadsden and Liberty counties.

Boundary between Gadsden and Liberty cos.

SECTION 1. *Be it enacted by the Senate and House of Representatives of the State of Florida in General Assembly convened*, That the present line, dividing Liberty and Gadsden counties, be changed and defined as follows, viz: Commence on the Ocklockonee river, at the mouth of Pittman's creek; thence up said creek to where the section line between ten and eleven, township one, South, range five, West, (United States Survey,) crosses said creek; thence on a line due North to Ocklawaha creek; thence along said creek to its source; thence due North to the present Rock Bluff or Federal road; thence along said road to where it crosses Mule creek; thence up said creek to its head; thence in a straight line to the head of the West prong of Crooked creek, or Edgerton's Mill creek; thence down said creek to township line between townships two and three, North; thence along said township line to the Apalachicola river.

Suits, where to be prosecuted.

SEC. 2. *Be it further enacted*, That all suits or actions in any of the Courts of Liberty or Gadsden to which any of the persons affected by the above alteration of boundary may be parties, shall be prosecuted and finally adjusted in the same manner as if this alteration had not been made.

Repeal.

SEC. 3. *Be it further enacted*, That all acts and parts of acts conflicting with the provisions of this act be and the same are hereby repealed.

Passed the House of Representatives December 22, 1859. Passed the Senate December 22, 1859. Approved by the Governor December 22, 1859.

CHAPTER 1,047—[No. 52.]

AN ACT to correct an error in a printed bill entitled an act to create the
counties of Suwannee and New River.

SECTION 1. *Be it enacted by the Senate and House of Representatives of the State of Florida in General Assembly convened,* That so much of the bill above entitled as calls for 6 per cent. upon railroad bonds from the citizens of Columbia, Suwannee and New River counties be struck out, and 8 per cent. inserted.

Error as to interest on railroad bonds corrected.

Passed the Senate December 5, 1859. Passed the House of Representatives December 10, 1859. Approved by the Governor December 19, 1859.

CHAPTER 1,048—[No. 53.]

AN ACT to change the boundary line between Columbia and Suwannee
Counties.

SECTION 1. *Be it enacted by the Senate and House of Representatives of the State of Florida in General Assembly convened,* That, from and after the passage of this act, the boundary line between Columbia and Suwannee counties shall commence at the mouth of Rocky creek, on the Suwannee river, lying between range line 15 and 16, run thence due South to the head of Itchetucknee and then down said stream to the Suwannee river.

Boundary between Columbia and Suwannee Counties.

SEC. 2. *Be it further enacted,* That all laws or parts of laws conflicting with the true intent and meaning of this act be and the same are hereby repealed.

Repeal.

Passed the Senate December 2, 1859. Passed the House of Representatives December 9, 1859. Approved by the Governor December 12, 1859.

CHAPTER 1,049—[No. 54.]

AN ACT to regulate the fees of Notary Publics in the county of St. Johns.

SECTION 1. *Be it enacted by the Senate and House of Representatives of the State of Florida in General Assem-*

1859.

Fees.

bly convened, That, from and after the passage of this act, the fees of Notary Publics of the county of St. Johns shall be the same amount as that which are now allowed by law to Notaries in the county of Monroe.

Passed the House of Representatives December 12th, 1859. Passed the Senate December 16, 1859. Approved by the Governor December 21, 1859.

CHAPTER 1,050—[No. 56.]

AN ACT to unite the offices of Judge of Probate and Clerk of the Circui in Volusia county.

Clerk to be ex-officio Judge of Probate.

SECTION 1. *Be it enacted by the Senate and House of Representatives of the State of Florida in General Assembly convened* That the Clerk of the Circuit Court in the county of Volusia shall hereafter be ex-officio Judge of Probate of said county, and shall perform the duties of the said offices respectively.

When act to take effect.

SEC. 2. *Be it further enacted,* That this act shall take effect only after the expiration of the present term of these offices, or in case of vacancy from any cause.

Repeal.

SEC. 3. *Be it further enacted,* That all laws and parts of laws conflicting with this act be and the same are hereby repealed.

Passed the House of Representatives December 8, 1859. Passed the Senate December 16, 1859. Approved by the Governor December 20, 1859.

CHAPTER 1,051—[No. 55.]

AN ACT for the benefit of the heirs of the estate of James E. Hendry, dec'd

Sale of land by adm'r confirmed

SECTION 1. *Be it enacted by the Senate and House of Representatives of the State of Florida in General Assembly convened,* That the real estate of James E. Hendry, late of Hillsborough county, deceased, sold at public outcry on the twelfth day of March, eighteen hundred and fifty-five, by Alderman Carlton, as administrator of said deceased, be and the same is hereby confirmed.

SEC. 2. *Be it further enacted,* That the administrator *de bonis non* of the said James E. Hendry, deceased, be and he is hereby authorized and required to make, execute, sign, seal and deliver as such administrator *de bonis non* of said James E. Hendry, dec'd, good and sufficient deed or deeds to the purchaser or purchasers of the real estate or lands sold on the day mentioned in the first section of this act by Alderman Carlton, as administrator of said deceased, and in case and if it should appear that any of said lands have been conveyed by the said purchaser or purchasers, then and in that case the said administrator *de bonis non* shall make good and sufficient deed or deeds to the assignee or assignees of such purchaser or purchasers: *Provided,* The purchaser or purchasers, assignee or assignees of such purchaser or purchasers, shall pay or cause to be paid to the administrator *de bonis non* of said James E. Hendry, for the use and benefit of the said James E. Hendry's estate, the purchase price per acre at which said land or lands sold for at the sale made by Alderman Carlton, administrator of said Hendry on the (12) twelfth day of March, eighteen hundred and fifty-five.

Adm'r de bonis non authorized to make title deeds to purchasers or their assigns.

Proviso.

Passed the House of Representatives December 20, 1859. Passed the Senate December 22, 1859. Approved by the Governor December 22, 1859.

CHAPTER 1,052—[No. 57.]

AN ACT for the relief of Noah P. Suggs of Lafayette county.

WHEREAS, Noah P. Suggs, of Lafayette county, being a cripple, and unable on that account to perform labor requiring the exercise of physical power; AND WHEREAS, He is desirous of exercising his faculties to honorably maintaining himself and family by occupying his time in peddling goods in Lafayette county, Florida, and being in such circumstances that he is unable to do so and pay the amount required by license—Therefore,

Preamble.

Be it enacted by the Senate and House of Representatives of the State of Florida in General Assembly convened, That Noah P. Suggs, of Lafayette county, is hereby authorized to peddle goods, wares and merchandize free from all charges for license in the county of Lafayette: *Provided,* It is done by himself in person and for his own profit, and not

Authorized to peddle without license in Lafayette County.

Proviso.

for the benefit, directly or indirectly, of other parties to enter into said business.

Passed the Senate December 3, 1859. Passed the House of Representatives December 8, 1859. Approved by the Governor December 19, 1859.

CHAPTER 1,053.—[No. 58.]

AN ACT for the relief of John M. Hill.

Preamble.

WHEREAS, John M. Hill, of Leon county, Florida, did obtain a license for retailing spiritous liquors for the year commencing on the first of October, 1859, and on the 20th of November ensuing his stock of liquors were destroyed by fire, together with the building in which they were kept; AND WHEREAS, By reason of said misfortune, the said John M. Hill represents himself as unable to resume the business of retailing spiritous liquors, and cannot therefore receive any further benefit from the license granted under the authority of the State—Therefore,

Amount to be refunded.

SECTION 1. *Be it enacted by the Senate and House of Representatives of the State of Florida in General Assembly convened,* That the amount of one hundred and seventy dollars and eighty-three cents be refunded to the said John M. Hill by the State of Florida, said amount being the sum paid for the license aforesaid, after deducting for the time when said John M. Hill exercised the business of retailing under said license.

When Compt'r to issue warrant and Treasurer to pay same.

SEC. 2. *Be it further enacted,* That if the Sheriff of Leon county has paid into the treasury of the State, or shall hereafter pay into the treasury of the State, the amount received from the said John M. Hill for said license, then the Comptroller of Public Accounts for the State is hereby authorized and required to issue a warrant upon the treasury in favor of said John M. Hill for the sum of one hundred and seventy dollars and eighty-three cents, and the Treasurer is hereby authorized and directed to pay the same. But if the Sheriff

Sheriff authorized to pay am't, when.

has not paid the moneys received by him for said license into the treasury of the State, then it shall be lawful for said Sheriff to refund to said John M. Hill the said amount of one hundred and seventy dollars and eighty-three cents; and upon the presentation by the Sheriff of Leon county of a receipt from said John M. Hill for said amount, the Comptroller is hereby authorized and required to credit said Sheriff with said amount on account of licenses: *Provided*, That said warrant shall not issue or said amount be refunded as aforesaid until the said John M. Hill shall surrender his license to the Sheriff of Leon county.

Passed the House of Representatives December 16, 1859. Passed the Senate December 22, 1859. Approved by the Governor December 22, 1859.

CHAPTER 1,054—[No. 59.]

AN ACT for the relief of John Addison and others.

SECTION 1. *Be it enacted by the Senate and House of Representatives of the State of Florida in General Assembly convened*, That the Governor of this State be and he is hereby authorized and requested to allow pay, rations, forage, &c., to Lieutenant John Addison, James Conliff, David N. Townsend, Cotton B. Rawls, John A. Addison, William H. Vanderipe, William H. Addison, David J. Addison, Joel J. Addison, Henry A. Clark, George H. Collins, John Craig, Jesse G. Gibson, William J. Gilly, Asa J. Goddard, William H. Harrison, Daniel L. Hawkins, William H. Johnston, Levin P. Johnston, Edward Marr, John L. McLean, Archibald McNeill, Daniel McMillan, John C. Myrick, Benjamin Oglesby, George Oglesby, Christian Peterson, Henry Peterson, William A. Rawls, James Vanderipe and James G. Williams from the sixteenth day of January, 1856, to the eighth day of April, 1856, as Mounted Volunteers, for services rendered and rations and forage furnished during said period in suppressing Indian hostilities in South Florida, said persons constituting a part of Lieutenant John Addison's detachment of Mounted Volunteers.

Governor authorized to allow pay rations, forage, &c., to Mounted Volunteers.

SEC. 2. *Be it further enacted*, That the Governor be and he is hereby authorized and requested to allow pay, rations, forage, &c., as Mounted Volunteers, to Joseph A. Braden and Isaiah Smith from the sixteenth day of January, 1856, to the seventh day of October, 1856, they being members of John Addison's detachment, and having served therein during said period: *Provided*, That their services shall be

Pay rations, &c., to J. A. Braden and I. Smith.

Proof to be made

10

proved to the satisfaction of the proper authority of this State.

Passed the House of Representatives December 22, 1859. Passed the Senate December 22, 1859. Approved December 22, 1859.

CHAPTER 1,055—[No. 60.]

AN ACT for the relief of Simeon A. Edwards.

WHEREAS, Captain L. Berry, of the steamer New Boston, and in the year A. D. 1856, a citizen of Florida, did in or about the month of June in said year transport in the said steamer from the town of New Boston, in the County of Columbia, to Bay Port in the County of Hernando, one Company, (foot) Florida Volunteers, under the command of Captain Alexander Bell, and did also furnish said Company with sufficient rations for their subsistence, having charged in the aggregate the sum of Three Hundred and Ten Dollars for said transportation and rations; *And Whereas,* The said Captain Bell certified to the justness and validity of the amount claimed by Captain Berry as due and owing by the State; *And Whereas,* The said Captain Berry transferred and delivered the said claim to one Simeon Edwards for a valuable consideration, and is now the legal and bona fide holder of the same, at the present time, *Therefore,*

SECTION 1. *Be it enacted by the Senate and House of Representatives of the State of Florida in General Assembly convened,* That the Governor be authorized, on the presentation of sufficient proofs, to pay the said account of Three Hundred and Ten Dollars out of any monies in his possession, or that may hereafter come into his possession applicable to transportation and subsistence of the volunteers, under the requisition of the Governor.

SEC. 2. *Be it further enacted,* That that the said Simeon A. Edwards be required to produce such evidence and proofs as the Comptroller of the State Accounts may in his judgment require.

Passed the House of Representatives December 16, 1859. Passed the Senate December 16, 1859. Approved by the Governor December 20, 1859.

Preamble.

Governor authorized to pay.

Out of what monies.

Proof to be made.

CHAPTER 1,056—[No. 61.]

AN ACT to correct an error in au act approved January 15th, 1859, entitled an act for the relief of Josiah Gates and other persons therein named, citizens of Manatee county.

SECTION 1. *Be it enacted by the Senate and House of Representatives of the State of Florida in General Assembly convened,* That the act approved January 15, 1859, entitled an act for the relief of Josiah Gates and other persons therein named, citizens of Manatee county, be amended by striking out the word "March" and inserting the word "April" in lieu thereof, the persons therein named having rendered services, as therein mentioned, from the sixteenth day of January, 1856, to the eighth of April, 1856, and having received no pay or emoluments therefor, and the said act having been by some error or mistake so drawn and passed as to allow them pay, &c., only until the eighth day of March, 1856. *Error corrected.*

Passed the House of Representatives December 17, 1859. Passed the Senate December 22, 1859. Approved by the Governor December 22, 1859.

CHAPTER 1,057—[No. 62.]

AN ACT for the relief of Samuel B. Williford, the County Surveyor of Jackson county.

SECTION 1. WHEREAS, Samuel B. Williford, the County Surveyor of Jackson county, did, at the instance and request of the Solicitor for the Western Circuit, survey a portion of the boundary line between the counties of Jackson, Washington and Calhoun, in order to determine the venue in a certain capital case in this State, which could not otherwise be ascertained on account of the indefiniteness of the said boundary line—Therefore, *Preamble.*

Be it enacted by the Senate and House of Representatives of the State of Florida in General Assembly convened, That the Comptroller be and he is hereby authorized to audit and allow the said Samuel B. Williford the sum of seventy-five 25-100 dollars for his services and necessary ex- *Amount to be audited by Comptroller and paid by Treas'r.*

LAWS OF FLORIDA.

penses in and about the said survey; and the Treasurer of the State is hereby required to pay the same.

Passed the House of Representatives December 9, 1859. Passed the Senate December 14, 1859. Approved by the Governor December 20, 1859.

CHAPTER 1,058.—[No. 63.]

AN ACT for the relief of H. T. Blocker.

Preamble.

WHEREAS, The said H. T. Blocker was Sheriff of Leon County when the sessions of the Supreme Court were held during the years from 1854 to 1857, inclusive; *and whereas*, Prior to 1854, and since 1857, the said Supreme Court allowed to the Sheriff of the county where its terms were held, a per diem of three dollars during the term of the Court although it was not in actual session every day of the time; *and whereas*, The Chief Justice of the Supreme Court has refused to allow to the said H. T. Blocker his per diem during the session of said Supreme Court between the years 1854 and 1857, inclusive; *and whereas*, The said H. T. Blocker was ordered by the said Supreme Court to summon the Hon. J. J. Finley, Judge of the Western Circuit, to attend a session of the Supreme Court at Tallahassee, and did summon said Judge to attend said Court, in doing which he incurred great expense and was put to great trouble, for which he charged the sum of fifty dollars, which was disallowed by said Chief Justice; Therefore,

Comptroller to audit account of, and Treasurer to pay.

SECTION 1. *Be it enacted by the Senate and House of Representatives of the State of Florida in General Assembly convened,* That the Comptroller audit and allow to the said H. T. Blocker, such sum as may be due him for such per diem, and for summoning said Judge, and that the Treasurer pay the same out of any money in the Treasury not otherwise appropriated.

Passed the House of Representatives December 12, 1859. Passed the Senate December 16, 1859. Approved by the Governor December 20, 1859.

CHAPTER 1,059—[No. 64.]

AN ACT for the relief of Allen Gibson, of Marion county, and Solomon F Haliday, of Alachua county.

WHEREAS, Allen Gibson and Solomon F. Haliday, of the counties of Marion and Alachua, did, during the month of January, 1857, furnish forage and subsistence to Captain Carter's Company of Mounted Volunteers; AND WHEREAS, Captain Carter represented that he was authorized by General Carter to procure forage and subsistence and that the State would pay for the same; AND WHEREAS, The same remains unpaid to the present time—Therefore, Preamble.

SECTION 1. *Be it enacted by the Senate and House of Representatives of the State of Florida in General Assembly convened*, That the Governor be and he is hereby authorized, on presentation of sufficient proof, to pay or cause to be paid their accounts, out of any moneys in his possession, or may hereafter come into his possession, applicable to forage and subsistence account for volunteer service of the State. Governor authorized to pay accounts of.
Out of what money.

SEC. 2. *Be it further enacted*, That the said Allen Gibson and Solomon F. Haliday be required to produce such evidence and before such tribunal as the Comptroller of Public Accounts may in his judgment require. Proof to be made.

Passed the Senate December 16, 1859. Passed the House of Representatives December 16, 1859. Approved by the Governor December 21, 1859.

CHAPTER 1,060—[No. 65.]

AN ACT for the relief of Matias F. Papy.

SECTION 1. *Be it enacted by the Senate and House of Representatives of the State of Florida in General Assembly convened*, That the Comptroller of Public Accounts is hereby authorized and required to issue his warrant on the Treasurer in favor of M. F. Papy for the sum of one hundred and seventy-one dollars, for balance of per diem due him Amount to be paid to.

and unpaid as Clerk of the Supreme Court, and the Treasurer is hereby authorized and required to pay the same.

Passed the House of Representatives December 12, 1859. Passed the Senate December 16, 1859. Approved by the Governor December 20, 1859.

CHAPTER 1,061—[No. 66.]

AN ACT for the relief of Andrew J. Moore and Wm. S. Dilworth.

[Comptroller, what to audit.]

SECTION 1. *Be it enacted by the Senate and House of Representatives of the State of Florida in General Assembly convened,* That the Comptroller be and he is hereby directed to audit and allow certificate number 316 of the State of Florida, for the sum of forty dollars and fifteen cents: *Provided,* That Andrew J. Moore and William S.

Proviso.

Dilworth shall enter into bond, payable to the Comptroller, in double the sum of said certificate, to refund the amount of said certificate, with interest thereon, should it hereafter appear that the endorsement of said certificate by J. P. McMullen for Malcomb Gillis was improperly made.

Passed the Senate December 6, 1859. Passed the House of Representatives December 12, 1859. Approved by the Governor December 19, 1859.

CHAPTER 1,062—[No. 67.]

AN ACT for the relief of Isaac N. Shepard, Guardian of the minor heirs of Henry M. Shepard, late of Gadsden County, deceased.

Preamble.

WHEREAS, Henry M. Shepard did in his life-time purchase of the late Hugh O. McLean, Tax Assessor and Collector of Gadsden County, a tract of land, to-wit: in the year A. D. 1851 ; said land having been sold for taxes, as the property of one Robert Jimerson, for which he paid forty-three dollars ; *and whereas,* The said Isaac is now the legally appointed Guardians of the said minor heirs ; *and whereas,* It has since appeared that said land did not belong to the said Jimerson, but was the property of another, and was sold as such, to-wit: on the 4th of February, 1857 : Therefore,

SECTION 1. *Be it enacted by the Senate and House of*

Representatives of the State of Florida in General Assembly convened, That the Comptroller of the State be authorized and directed to audit, and the Treasurer to pay the claim of the said Isaac N. Shepard, guardian, as aforesaid, for the sum of forty-seven dollars and ninety-eight cents, being the amount with interest from February 4th, 1857, improperly paid out by the said Henry M. Shepard, as stated in the above preamble.

Amount to be audited & paid to.

Passed the House of Representatives December 10, 1859. Passed the Senate December 21, 1859. Approved by the Governor December 20, 1859.

CHAPTER 1,063—[No. 68.]

AN ACT for the relief of Isaac N. Shepard of Gadsden County.

WHEREAS, Isaac N. Shepard of Gadsden County purchased of the late Hugh O. McLean, Tax Assessor and Collector of said County, a tract of land in the year A. D. 1852, said land having been sold for taxes as the property of one Robert Jimerson, for which he paid twenty-one dollars and seventy-four cents ; *and whereas,* The said Shepard did in the year A. D. 1854, purchase of James M. Smith, late Tax Assessor and Collector of said County, another tract of land which was sold for taxes, as the property of the said Jimerson for which he paid seventeen dollars and sixty-eight cents; *and whereas,* It has since appeared that said lands did not belong to the said Jimerson, but were the property of another person from whom the said Shepard, to-wit : on the 4th day of February, 1857, purchased the same : Therefore,

Preamble.

SECTION 1. *Be it enacted by the Senate and House of Representatives of the State of Florida in General Assembly convened,* That the Comptroller of the State be, and he is hereby authorized and directed to audit, and the Treasurer to pay the claim of Isaac N. Shepard of Gadsden county, for the sum of forty-nine dollars and fifty-one cents, being the amount with interest, from February 4th, 1857, improperly paid out by the said Shepard, as stated in the above preamble.

Amount to be audited & paid to.

Passed the House of Representatives December 10, 1859. Passed the Senate December 15, 1859. Approved by the Governor December 20, 1859.

CHAPTER 1,064—[No. 69.]

AN ACT for the relief of Susan Pearce, administratrix, and James T. Lester, administrator of the estate of William Pearce.

Amount to be paid to.

SECTION 1. *Be it enacted by the Senate and House of Representatives of the State of Florida in General Assembly convened,* That there be paid, out of any money in the Treasury not otherwise appropriated, the sum of five hundred and twenty-five dollars and fifty cents, being one-half of the value of a negro man named Hall, who killed his master, the said William Pearce, and was afterwards hung therefor.

Passed the House of Representatives December 20, 1859. Passed the Senate December 22, 1859. Approved by the Governor December 22, 1859.

CHAPTER 1,065—[No. 70.]

AN ACT for the relief of Harrison Fairbank.

Authorized to build a grist mill

Proviso.

SECTION 1. *Be it enacted by the Senate and House of Representatives of the State of Florida in General Assembly convened,* That the said Harrison Fairbank be authorized to build a grist mill on the waters of the Ocklockonee: *Provided,* That said mill be made in a substantial manner and shall be subject to the rules and regulations now provided by law.

Passed the House of Representatives December 16, 1859. Passed the Senate December 20, 1859. Approved by the Governor December 22, 1859.

CHAPTER 1,066—[No. 71.]

AN ACT to establish a Ferry across the Ocklawaha river.

Authorized to establish ferry.

SECTION 1. *Be it enacted by the Senate and House of Representatives of the State of Florida in General Assembly convened,* That John W. Pearson be and he is hereby authorized to establish a ferry across the Ocklawaha river, in Marion county, at the mouth of Orange creek, for

and during the term of twenty years from the passage of
this act.

SEC. 2. *Be it further enacted*, That the said John W.
Pearson, his heirs and assigns, shall at all times keep a good
and sufficient ferry-boat or flat, for the crossing of all ne-
groes, carts, carriages, cattle and other stock, and he shall
receive such rates of ferriage as shall or may be established
from time to time by the County Commissioners of the
county of Marion, and be subject to the order of said Commissioners.

SEC. 3. *Be it further enacted*, That if the said John W.
Pearson shall fail to establish the said ferry within one year
from the passage of this act, then the rights and privileges
granted by this act be void.

On failure to es-
tablish   ferry
within one year,
privilege forfeit-
ed.

Passed the Senate December 6, 1859. Passed the House of Representatives
December 12, 1859. Approved by the Governor December 19, 1859.

CHAPTER 1,067—[No. 72.]

AN ACT to authorize Spencer Price of Levy County, to establish a Ferry
from Number Four on the main land, to the Western terminus of the Florida Railroad on Way Key, thence across the Bay to the city of Atseena Otie.

SECTION 1. *Be it enacted by the Senate and House of
Representatives of the State of Florida in General Assembly convened,* That Spencer Price be, and he is hereby
authorized to establish a Ferry from No. Four on the main
land, to the Western terminus of the Florida Railroad on
Way Key, thence across the bay to the city of Atseena-Otie,
for and during the term of ten years.

SEC. 2. *Be it further enacted*, That if the said Spencer
Price, his heirs and assigns, shall establish a Ferry from Number Four on the main land, to the Western terminus of the
Florida Railroad on Way Key, and from thence across the
bay to the city of Atseena-Otie, and keep always in readiness
a good and sufficient boat or flat for crossing wagons and
teams, carts and carriages, cattle and other live stock in safe-
ty, within six months from the passage of this act, then this
act shall be in full force and effect, otherwise the same to be
null and void.

SEC. 3. *Be it further enacted*, That the rates of ferriage

11

LAWS OF FLORIDA.

shall be regulated by the County Commissioners of Levy County.

Passed the Senate December 7, 1859. Passed the House of Representatives December 12th, 1859. Approved by the Governor December 16, 1859.

CHAPTER 1,068—[No. 73.]

AN ACT to authorize Geo. W. Martin to establish a Ferry across the Suwannee River at Fayetteville.

Authorized to establish ferry.

SECTION 1. *Be it enacted by the Senate and House of Representatives of the State of Florida in General Assembly convened,* That Geo. W. Martin be, and he is hereby authorized to establish a Ferry across the Suwannee River at Fayetteville.

Within what time to be established.

SEC. 2. *Be it further enacted,* That if the said Geo. W. Martin, his heirs and assigns, shall establish a Ferry across the Suwannee River at Fayetteville, sufficiently safe for the crossing of loaded wagons and teams, cattle and other stock, within three months from the passage of this act, then this act shall be in full force and effect, otherwise the same to be null and void.

Rates of ferriage

SEC. 3. *Be it further enacted,* That the rates of crossing persons at said Ferry shall be regulated by the County Commissioners of Lafayette County.

Passed the Senate December 3, 1859. Passed the House of Representatives December 16, 1859. Approved by the Governor December 22, 1859.

CHAPTER 1,069—[No. 74.]

AN ACT to allow William W. Tucker of Jefferson County, to assume the management of his own estate.

Authorized to assume management of estate.

SECTION 1. *Be it enacted by the Senate and House of Representatives of the State of Florida in General Assembly convened,* That William W. Tucker, a minor, of Jefferson County, of this State, be, and he is hereby authorized and empowered to assume the management and control of his estate.

SEC. 2. *Be it further enacted,* That all receipts, bonds,

obligations, or contracts of whatever nature hereafter given, made or entered into by him, the said William W. Tucker, shall be, and are hereby declared as valid and binding in Law or Equity, as if the same had been given, made or entered into after he had attained the age of twenty-one years, and he is hereby made capable of suing and being sued, of pleading and being impleaded in any Court of Law or Equity in this State.

Contracts. &c. of to be binding.

May sue and be sued.

Passed the House of Representatives December 7, 1859. Passed the Senate December 15, 1859. Approved by the Governor December 20, 1859.

CHAPTER 1,070—[No. 75.]

AN ACT to authorize Joseph D. Smith to assume the management of his own Estate.

SECTION 1. *Be it enacted by the Senate and House of Representatives of the State of Florida in General Assembly convened,* That Joseph D. Smith, a minor, be, and he is hereby authorized to assume the management of his own estate.

Authorized to assume management of estate.

SEC. 2. *Be it further enacted,* That the said Joseph D. Smith be and he is hereby empowered to contract and be contracted with, and all contracts entered into by him shall be as valid and binding in law as if he had attained to the age of twenty-one years.

Contracts of to be binding.

Passed the Senate December 16, 1859. Passed the House of Representatives December 17, 1859. Approved December 21, 1859.

CHAPTER 1,071—[No. 76.]

AN ACT to authorize Edmond N. Everitt, of Washington county, to assume the management of his own property.

SECTION 1. *Be it enacted by the Senate and House of Representatives of the State of Florida in General Assembly convened,* That Edmond N. Everitt, of Washington county, Florida, be and he is hereby authorized to assume the control and management of his own property of every kind, and that all contracts and arrangements hereafter

Authorized to assume management of estate.

Contracts to be binding.

made by the said Edmond N. Everitt be and the same are hereby declared to be as binding upon him as the same would be were he of lawful age.

Passed the Senate December 9, 1859. Passed the House of Representatives December 10, 1859. Approved by the Governor December 19, 1859.

CHAPTER 1,072—[No. 77.]

AN ACT to authorize William F. Green, of Gadsden county, to contract and be contracted with.

May contract & contracts to be binding.

SECTION 1. *Be it enacted by the Senate and House of Representatives of the State of Florida in General Assembly convened*, That from and after the passage of this act William F. Green, of Gadsden county, be and he is hereby empowered to contract and be contracted with, and to do all other acts in the transaction of business with the same validity and as fully, and to the same extent, as if he had attained to the age of twenty-one years.

Passed the Senate December 5, 1859. Passed the House of Representatives December 9, 1859. Approved by the Governor December 19, 1859.

CHAPTER 1,073—[No. 78.]

AN ACT to empower John W. Broxson and Isaac Broxson to assume the management of their own estates.

Authorized to assume management of estate.

Contracts to be binding.

SECTION 1. *Be it enacted by the Senate and House of Representatives of the State of Florida in General Assembly convened*, That John W. Broxson and Isaac Broxson be and they are hereby authorized to assume the control and management of their own estates, and that all contracts and agreements made hereafter by the said John W. Broxson and Isaac Broxson respectively be and the same are hereby declared to be as binding upon them as the same would be were they of lawful age.

Passed the Senate December 8, 1859. Passed the House of Representatives December 12, 1859. Approved by the Governor December 19, 1859.

CHAPTER 1,074—[No. 79.]

AN ACT to empower Littleberry Manning, a minor, to assume the management of his own estate.

SECTION 1. *Be it enacted by the Senate and House of Representatives of the State of Florida in General Assembly convened*, That Littleberry Manning, a minor, of Leon county, in this State, be and he is hereby authorized and empowered to assume the management of his own estate.

Authorized to assume management of estate.

SEC. 2. *Be it further enacted*, That all receipts, bonds, obligations or contracts, of whatsoever nature, hereafter given, made or entered into by him shall be and are hereby declared as valid and binding in law or equity as if the same had been given, made or entered into after he had attained the age of twenty-one years; and he is hereby made capable of suing and being sued, of pleading and being impleaded in any Court of law or equity in this State.

Contracts to be binding.

May sue and be sued.

Passed the House of Reprctentatives December 9, 1859. Passed the Senate December 12, 1859. Approved by the Governor December 20, 1859.

CHAPTER 1,075—[No. 80.]

AN ACT to empower Charles Maltbie West, a minor, of Leon county, to assume the management of his own estate.

SECTION 1. *Be it enacted by the Senate and House of Representatives of the State of Florida in General Assembly convened*, That Charles Maltbie West, a minor, of Leon county, in this State, be and he is hereby authorized and empowered to assume the management of his own estate.

Authorized to assume management of estate.

SEC. 2. *Be it further enacted*, That all receipts, bonds, obligations or contracts, of whatsoever nature, hereafter given, made or entered into by him, the said Charles Maltbie West, shall be and are hereby declared as valid and binding in law and equity as if the same had been given, made or entered into after he had attained the age of twenty-one years; and he is hereby made capable of suing and being sued, of pleading and being impleaded, in any Court of law or equity in this State.

Contracts to be binding.

May sue and be sued.

Passed the House of Representatives December 7, 1859. Passed the Senate December 17, 1859. Approved by the Governor December 20, 1859.

86

LAWS OF FLORIDA.

1859.

CHAPTER 1,076—[No. 81.]

AN ACT to authorize John S. Addison, a minor, of Marion county, to assume the management of his own estate.

Authorized to assume management of estate. SECTION 1. *Be it enacted by the Senate and House of Representatives of the State of Florida in General Assembly convened,* That John S. Addison, a minor, of Marion county, be and he is hereby authorized and empowered to assume the management of his own estate.

Contracts of to be binding. SEC. 2. *Be it further enacted,* That the said John S. Addison be and he is hereby empowered to contract and be contracted with, and all contracts entered into by him after the passage of this act, and all agreements or other engagements, shall be as valid and binding in law as if he had attained to the age of twenty-one years.

Passed the House of Representatives December 6, 1859. Passed the Senate December 8, 1859. Approved by the Governor December 19, 1859.

CHAPTER 1,077—[No. 82.]

AN ACT to empower David Franklin Houck to assume the management of his own estate.

Authorized to assume management of estate. SECTION 1. *Be it enacted by the Senate and House of Representatives of the State of Florida in General Assembly convened,* That David Franklin Houck, a minor, of Leon county, in this State, be and he is hereby authorized and empowered to assume the management and control of his own estate.

Contracts, &c. to be binding. SEC. 2. *Be it further enacted,* That all receipts, bonds, obligations or contracts, of whatsoever nature, hereafter given, made or entered into by him, the said David Franklin Houck, shall be and are hereby declared as valid and binding in law or equity as if the same had been given, made or entered into after he had attained the age of twen- **May sue and be sued.** ty-one years; and he is hereby made capable of suing and being sued, of pleading and being impleaded in any Court of law or equity in this State.

Passed the House of Representatives December 7, 1859. Passed the Senate December 17, 1859. Approved by the Governor December 21, 1859.

CHAPTER 1,078—[No. 83.]

AN ACT to authorize Minor W. Walker, of Jefferson county, to assume the management of his own estate.

SECTION 1. *Be it enacted by the Senate and House of Representatives of the State of Florida in General Assembly convened,* That Minor W. Walker, of Jefferson county, of this State, be and he is hereby authorized and empowered to assume the management and control of his own estate. *(Authorized to assume management of estate.)*

SEC. 2. *Be it further enacted,* That all receipts, bonds, obligations or contracts, of whatever nature, hereafter given, made or entered into by him, the said Minor W. Walker, shall be and are hereby declared as valid and binding in law or equity as if the same had been given, made or entered into after he had attained the age of twenty-one years; and he is hereby made capable of suing and being sued, of pleading and being impleaded in any Court of law or equity in this State. *(Contracts, &c. to be binding.) (May sue and be sued.)*

Passed the House of Representatives December 6th, 1859. Passed the Senate December 7, 1859. Approved by the Governor December 19, 1859.

CHAPTER 1,079—[No. 84.]

AN ACT to empower Susan M. Croom, a minor, of Leon county, to assume the management of her own estate.

SECTION 1. *Be it enacted by the Senate and House of Representatives of the State of Florida in General Assembly convened,* That Susan M. Croom, a minor, of Leon county, in this State, be and she is hereby authorized and empowered to assume the management of her own estate. *(Authorized to assume management of estate.)*

SEC. 2. *Be it further enacted,* That all receipts, bonds, obligations or contracts, of whatever kind or nature, hereafter given, made or entered into by her, the said Susan M. Croom, shall be and are hereby declared as valid and binding in law and equity as if the same had been given, made and entered into after she had attained the age of twenty-one years; and she is hereby made capable of suing and be- *(Contracts, &c. to be binding.) (May sue and be sued.)*

ing sued, of pleading and being impleaded in any Court of law or equity in this State.

Passed the House of Representatives December 7, 1859. Passed the Senate December 15, 1859. Approved by the Governor December 17, 1859.

CHAPTER 1,080—[No. 85.]

AN ACT to empower Thomas J. Chace, a minor, of Jefferson county, to assume the management of his own estate.

Authorized to assume management of estate.

SECTION 1. *Be it enacted by the Senate and House of Representatives of the State of Florida in General Assembly convened* That Thomas J. Chace, a minor, be and he is hereby authorized and empowered to assume the management and control of his own estate.

Contracts, &c. of be binding

SEC. 2. *Be it further enacted,* That all receipts, bonds, obligations or contracts, of every character, hereafter given, made or entered into by him, the said Thomas J. Chace, shall be and are hereby declared as valid and binding in law or equity as if the same had been given, made or entered into after he had attained the age of twenty-one years;

May sue and be sued.

and he is hereby made capable of suing and being sued in any Court of law or equity in this State, the same as if he had attained the age of twenty-one years.

Passed the House of Representatives December 14, 1859. Passed the Senate December 17, 1859. Approved by the Governor December 21, 1859.

CHAPTER 1,081—[No. 86.]

AN ACT to authorize Daniel Newnan Cone, a minor, of Columbia county, to assume the management of his own estate.

Authorized to assume management of estate.

SECTION 1. *Be it enacted by the Senate and House of Representatives of the State of Florida in General Assembly convened,* That, from and after the passage of this act, Daniel Newnan Cone, of Columbia county, shall be authorized to assume the management of his own estate.

SEC. 2. *Be it further enacted,* That all contracts entered

into by the said Daniel Newnan Cone shall be as binding as if he had attained the age of twenty-one years.

Passed the Senate December 17, 1859. Passed the House of Representatives December 21, 1859. Approved by the Gevernor December 22, 1859.

CHAPTER 1,082—[No. 87.]

AN ACT to change the name of George Frisby.

SECTION 1. *Be it enacted by the Senate and House of Representatives of the State of Florida in General Assembly convened*, That, from and after the passage of this act, the name of George Frisby shall be changed to that of George Reuben Frisby.

Name changed.

Passed the House of Representatives December 6, 1859. Passed the Senate December 9, 1859. Approved by the Governor December 19, 1859.

CHAPTER 1,083—[No. 88.]

AN ACT to change the name of George Gibbs Smith.

SECTION 1. *Be it enacted by the Senate and House of Representatives of the State of Florida in General Assembly convened*, That the name of George Gibbs Smith be and the same is hereby changed to George Garey Smith.

Name changed.

Passed the House of Representatives December 6, 1859. Passed the Senate December 9, 1859. Approved December 19, 1859.

CHAPTER 1,084—[No. 89.]

AN ACT to change the name of Hugh Martin Newsoms to Hugh Martin Keen.

SECTION 1. *Be it enacted by the Senate and House of Representatives of the State of Florida in General Assembly convened*, That, from and after the passage of this act,

Name changed:

12

the name of Hugh Martin Newsoms, of Columbia county, be changed to Hugh Martin Keen.

Passed the Senate December 6, 1859. Passed the House of Representatives December 9, 1859. Approved by the Governor December 19, 1859.

CHAPTER 1,085.—[No. 90.]

AN ACT to change the name of Mary King to Mary Hancock.

SECTION 1. *Be it enacted by the Senate and House of* Name changed. *Representatives of the State of Florida in General Assembly convened,* That, from and after the passage of this act, the name of Mary King, of Lake City, Columbia county, be and the same is hereby changed to that of Mary Hancock.

Passed the Senate December 6, 1859. Passed the House of Representatives December 9, 1859. Approved by the Governor December 19, 1859.

CHAPTER 1,086—[No. 91.]

AN ACT to change the name of Andrew J. Revells, of Madison county, to that of Andrew J. Duncan.

SECTION 1. *Be it enacted by the Senate and House of Representatives of the State of Florida in General Assem-* Name changed. *bly convened,* That, from and after the passage of this act, the name of Andrew J. Revells, of Madison county, be and the same is hereby changed to that of Andrew J. Duncan, and that hereafter he shall be entitled to said name of Andrew J. Duncan.

Passed the House of Representatives December 7, 1859. Passed the Senate December 15, 1859. Approved by the Governor December 20, 1859.

CHAPTER 1,087—[No. 92.]

AN ACT for the relief of Alexander Douglass, Peter C. Williams and Kenner McCaskil.

SECTION 1. *Be it enacted by the Senate and House of Rep-*

resentatives of the State of Florida in General Assembly convened, That the Comptroller of Public Accounts be and is hereby authorized to audit and allow the following accounts, viz: To Alexander Douglass, the sum of seventy-eight 25-100 dollars, ($78 25;) to Peter C. Williams, M. D., the sum of thirty-five dollars; to Kenneth McCaskil, the sum of sixty-seven dollars, the said sums of money respectively being expended by the above-named persons in the arrest, confinement, board and medical attendance upon one Leonard Singletery.

Amounts to be audited by Comptroller.

Passed the House of Representatives December 6, 1859. Passed the Senate December 17, 1859. Approved by the Governor December 20, 1859.

CHAPTER 1,093—[No. 88.]

AN ACT making appropriations for the expenses of the State Government for the fiscal years of 1859 and 1860.

SECTION 1. *Be it enacted by the Senate and House of Representatives of the State of Florida in General Assembly convened*, That the Comptroller of the State be required to issue Warrants to the following persons, viz:

Appropriation for expenses of Legislature.

J. Finlayson, President of the Senate,	-	$268
J. McRobert Baker,	- - -	201
A. S. Baldwin,	- - - -	165
George W. Call,	- - - -	181
D. C. Dawkins,	- - - -	117
Philip Dell,	- - - -	169
W. J. J. Duncan,	- - -	128
T. J. Eppes,	- - - -	175
J. Eubanks,	- - - -	228
G. D. Fisher,	- - - -	210
G. E. Hawes,	- - - -	210
W. B. Jones,	- - - -	138
W. J. Keitt,	- - - -	186
T. B. Lamar,	- - - -	77
W. W. McCall,	- - - -	145
L. G. McElvy,	- - - -	89
J. W. McQueen,	- - - -	150
A. W. Nicholson,	- - -	228
H. H. Walker,	- - - -	88

I. Welch,	171
F. Watlington,	296
Jas. E. Bowden, Secretary of Senate,	125
Jacob Gibson, Ass't " "	125
E. M. West. Enrolling Clerk,	115
H. Black, Engrossing Clerk,	100
S. J. Pittman, Sergeant-at-arms,	100
J. White, Door-Keeper,	125
Dr. DuBose, Chaplain,	50
J. B. Galbraith, Speaker House of Representatives,	240
F. C. Barrett,	175
D. B. Bird,	90
Theo. Bissell,	455
T. W. Brevard,	75
C. Brinson,	125
C. L. Broxson,	165
A. Bush,	111
A. Campbell,	106
J. B. Christie,	80
L. A. Church,	106
J. J. Clvatt,	161
C. C. Coffee,	106
R. H. M. Davidson,	86
J. M. F. Irwin,	111
S. Evans,	146
J. Frink,	125
J. Gettis,	275
C. Gillis,	210
J. S. Heermans,	356
Thos. Hughey,	275
Thos. Hunt,	175
T. Ingram,	175
J. Johnston,	197
D. L. Kenan,	86
J. D. Leigh,	210
A. M. Manning,	90
M. J. McKinnon,	150
A. McNeill,	270
J. A. Mickler,	186
R. D. Munn,	175
N. Nicks,	225
R. M. Peacock,	131
T. J. M. Richardson,	85

S. Roberts,	- - - -	145
I. C. Robinson,	- - - -	111
J. G. Smith,	- - - -	176
J. W. Starke,	- - - -	251
D. A. Vogt,	- - - -	186
S. White,	- - - -	106
G. Whitfield,	- - - -	90
J. Wiggins,	- - - -	191
W. J. Williams,	- - -	255
R. C. Williams,	- - - -	80
J. Yon,	- - - -	106
E. M. Graham, Chief Clerk,	- -	125
M. F. Papy, Ass't "	- -	106
R. L. Bruce, " "	- -	24
S. B. Shchee, Sergeant-at-Arms,	- -	100
G. W. Floyd, Messenger,	- -	100
Wm. Rowell, Door-Keeper,	- -	100
Jas. Hudson, Enrolling Clerk,	- -	100
William McIntosh, Engrossing Clerk,	-	10)
F. A. Branch, Chaplain,	- - -	50
H. Hawkins, servant,	- - -	25
C. H. Fisher, for ringing bell,	- -	10

For Hart & Barefoot, Editors of the Sentinel,
and Dyke & Carlisle, Editors of the Floridian,
and for miscellaneous printing, journals, laws
and general laws for distribution, passed at the
present session, $4,500 00

For McDougall & Hobby, stationery and candles, and for contingent items of this session, 455 58

Sec. 2. *Be it further enacted*, That the following sums be and they are hereby appropriated for the fiscal year 1860, to wit:

For salaries of public officers,	- -	$29,900
For jurors and State witnesses,	- -	30,000
For criminal prosecutions and contingent expenses of Circuit Courts,	- - -	17,000
For contingent expenses of State,	- -	5,000
For contingent expenses of Supreme Court,	-	2,000
For interest of State debt,	- -	27,000
For maintainance of lunatics,	- -	3,000
For residence of Governor,	- -	500
For post mortem examinations,	- -	500
For Presidential election,	- -	800

For repairs of Capitol and necessary fixtures, -   2,000
For Judge J. W. Baker, for extra judicial services
   in the Supreme Court,   -   -   400
For Judge Thomas F. King, for extra judicial ser-
   vices in the Supreme Court,   -   -   400
For writing up House journals of 1858 and '59,   200

Passed the Senate December 22, 1859. Passed the House of Representatives December 22, 1859. Approved by the Governor December 22, 1859.

RESOLUTIONS

Passed at an Adjourned Session of the General Assembly,

1859.

[No. 1.]

RESOLUTION relative to the Common School Laws.

Resolved, That the State Superintendent of Common Schools be and he is hereby directed to have five hundred copies of the act entitled an act to establish Common Schools, and to repeal certain acts in relation thereto, approved January 15th, 1853, printed, and to forward for distribution to each of the Judges of Probate in the State their equal proportion of said act.

School Law to be published for distribution.

Passed the House of Representatives December 20, 1859. Passed the Senate December 22, 1859. Approved by the Governor December 22, 1859.

[No. 2.]

RESOLUTION relative to the establishment of the boundary line between the State of Georgia and the State of Florida.

Resolved by the Senate and House of Representatives of the State of Florida in General Assembly convened, That, on the final designation and establishment of the boundary line between the States of Florida and Georgia, if any land shall fall within the jurisdiction of this State the title to which may have been conveyed or granted by Georgia, and which land shall, by virtue of any act of the Congress of the United States or otherwise, enure to this State, the Governor of this State is and shall be authorized and empowered to surrender to such person as may *bona fide* hold the title from Georgia all interest which this State may have therein.

Governor authorized to surrender title of State to Land held under authority of Georgia, when.

To unite with
Georgia in ap-
plication to Gen-
eral Governm'nt
to secure land
to holders from
Georgia.

Be it further resolved, That the Governor is hereby authorized to unite with the authorities of Georgia in any application to the General Government for such measures as may be deemed best to secure the *bona fide* holders of land the title which they may have derived from the State of Georgia.

May direct nolle
pros. to be enter-
ed, when.

Be it further resolved, That, in the event of any criminal prosecutions arising out of any difficulties between the persons residing in the disputed territory, the Governor is hereby authorized, in his judgment, to direct *nolle prosequis* to be entered and to take such other steps or measures as he may deem proper to preserve kindly relations between the people of the two States.

Passed the Senate December 3, 1859. Passed the House of Representatives December 12, 1859. Approved by the Governor December 19, 1859.

[No. 3.]

JOINT RESOLUTION with regard to certain persons who have circulated, or aided in circulating, an incendiary publication called The Impending Crisis of the South.

Preamble.

WHEREAS, A treasonable book, which is entitled "Compendium of the Impending Crisis of the South," said to be by Hinton Rowan Helper, of North Carolina, has been circulated in the State of Florida, and has been published with design and circulated with intent to create a revolt or insurrection of slaves in the State of Florida; AND WHEREAS, We are informed that certain members of Congress have aided and assisted in circulating this book in the Southern States and in Florida, by furnishing money and in other respects aiding the circulation of the same, thereby attempting to incite a revolt of slaves, which offence, although not committed in person by them, has been, through the assistance of the United States mail, consummated in Florida, so far as the delivery of the same is concerned, but the act, if done in this State, would, when proven under indictment, result in a sentence of death, it being a matter of doubt whether such person or persons who are principals or accomplices in the circulating this book from out of the jurisdiction of Florida can be tried by our Courts; AND WHEREAS, Those members of

Congress have committed an act which, if our Courts had jurisdiction of their persons, would subject them to suffer death for an attempt at inciting revolt or insurrection among slaves in Florida—Therefore,

Be it resolved by the Senate and House of Representatives of the State of Florida in General Assembly convened, That our Senators and Representative in Congress be and they are hereby instructed that they immediately prefer charges against each and every member of the Congress of the United States who have in any manner whatever aided in sending to or in circulating in the State of Florida a book called "Compendium of the Impending Crisis of the South," said to be by Hinton Rowan Helper, of North Carolina, thereby attempting to incite a revolt of slaves, and demand the expulsion of such member who shall be found guilty of so doing.

Senators and Rep. in Congress instructed to prefer charges.

Passed the House of Representatives December 19, 1859. Passed the Senate December 21, 1859. Approved December 22, 1859.

[No. 4.]

RESOLUTION to empower the Governor of the State to sell certain bonds.

Be it resolved by the Senate and House of Representatives of the State of Florida in General Assembly convened, That the Governor of the State be and he is hereby authorized and empowered to sell, at their fair market value, such an amount of the bonds that were issued in pursuance of an act in addition to an act to provide for the payment of the debts of the State, approved December 27th, 1857, as may be necessary to repay the loan for which the said bonds were hypothecated.

Governor authorized to sell bonds to pay loan for which they were pledged

Passed the Senate December 13, 1859. Passed the House of Representatives December 15, 1859. Approved by the Governor December 21, 1859.

[No. 5.]

RESOLUTION for the relief of the Comptroller of the State.

WHEREAS, By an act of the Legislature of this State to au-
13

Preamble.

thorise the business of banking, approved January 3d, 1853, and by act of the last session amendatory thereto, onerous and responsible duties are imposed on the Comptroller, making it his duty to receive securities and issue bills, bearing his signature, to a large amount for the several banking companies therein named, for which he receives no compensation—Therefore,

Comptroller authorized to accept compensation from Banks for services rendered.

Be it resolved by the Senate and House of Representatives of the State of Florida in General Assembly convened, That the Comptroller of this State be authorized to receive and accept from either or all the Banks of this State such compensation as they may think proper to make for the services which he has rendered them as Comptroller of this State.

Passed the House of Representatives December 8, 1859. Passed the Senate December 9, 1859. Approved by the Governor December 20, 1859.

[No. 6.]

RESOLUTION relative to the office of Register of U. S. Lands at Tallahassee.

Preamble.

WHEREAS, It is of much convenience and greatly facilitates the transaction of business in the Land Offices of the State that they should be near and accessible to the U. S. Land Office, and it is thus of advantage to the State and to the citizens thereof that the room in the Capitol now occupied by the Register of United States Lands, at Tallahassee, should be continued to be occupied by him—Therefore,

Register authorized to occupy room free of charge.

Be it resolved by the Senate and House of Representatives of the State of Florida in General Assembly convened, That the said U. S. Register be and he is hereby authorized to occupy said room free of charge or rent, and any sum which may be now due for rent from him for said room be and the same is hereby remitted.

Passed the House of Representatives December 8, 1859. Passed the Senate December 14, 1859. Approved by the Governor December 20, 1859.

[No. 7.]

RESOLUTION to change Mail Route No. 6,543.

WHEREAS, It has been made manifest that the extension of the mail route No. 6,543, from Atseena Otie, along the Gulf coast of Florida, to Clear Water Harbor, has been productive of little or no benefit to that portion of country, *Preamble.* owing to the sparseness of its population, and from other provisions having been made for a mail once a week sufficient for the wants of its few inhabitants; AND WHEREAS, Great advantages would result to a large extent of a more populous region by transferring that portion of such route to St. Marks—Therefore,

Be it resolved by the Senate and House of Representatives of the State of Florida in General Assembly convened, That our delegation in Congress be respectfully requested to urge upon the Post Office Department a change, which, besides conferring the benefits here pointed out, without detriment to other sections, would very considerably increase the postal receipts without any additional expense of transportation. *Delegation in Congress requested to procure change of Mail route.*

Passed the Senate December 15, 1859. Passed the House of Representatives December 17, 1859. Approved by the Governor December 21, 1859.

[No. 8.]

RESOLUTION urging upon Congress to establish a Fort and other necessary Fortifications.

Be it resolved by the Senate and House of Representatives of the State of Florida in General Assembly convened, That our Senators in Congress be instructed and our member requested to obtain the passage of an act to establish a Fort and other necessary fortifications at the port of Apalachicola and in said city of Apalachicola, in this State, and to urge appropriations from the Federal Government for that purpose. *Requesting Congress to establish Fortifications at Apalachicola, &c.*

Passed the Senate December 16, 1859. Passed the House of Representatives December 20, 1859. Approved by the Governor December 22, 1859.

[No. 9.]

JOINT RESOLUTION allowing the claims of Capt. Thomas Hughey.

Preamble.

WHEREAS, A joint resolution allowing the claims of Captain Thomas Hughey did receive the sanction of the Senatorial branch of the General Assembly of this State, and certified the same through their Secretary to this branch of the General Assembly, on the thirteenth day of January, eighteen hundred and fifty-nine; AND WHEREAS, The said joint resolution has been lost or mislaid, so that it cannot be found—Therefore,

Claimed allow'd

Be it resolved by the Senate and House of Representatives of the State of Florida in General Assembly convened, That the claim of Captain Hughey for transportation of troops in the service of the State, in the year (1856,) to the amount of eighty-eight 75-100 dollars, be and the same is hereby allowed to be just, and on presentation of his proof to the proper officer, the Paymaster is hereby authorized to audit and pay the same, with interest from date of service.

Paymaster to pay with interest.

Passed the Senate December 19, 1859. Passed the House of Representatives December 21, 1859. Approved by the Governor December 22, 1859.

[No. 10.]

RESOLUTION for the relief of Donald Cameron.

Appropriation.

Be it resolved by the Senate and House of Representatives of the State of Florida in General Assembly convened, That the sum of seventy dollars be appropriated by this General Assembly to Donald Cameron for writing up the Journal of last session and present session by order of the House.

Passed the House of Representatives December 22, 1859. Passed the Senate December 22, 1859. Approved by the Governor December 22, 1859.

[No. 11.]

RESOLUTION authorizing the Treasurer to pay Fifty Dollars for writing up the Journals of the Senate.

Resolved, That the Treasurer be and he is hereby authorized to pay J. E. Bowden, or such person as he may employ, the sum of Fifty Dollars, for writing up the Journals of the Senate.

Treasurer to pay to J. E. Bowden.

Passed the Senate December 22, 1859. Passed the House of Representatives December 22, 1859. Approved by the Governor December 22, 1859.

[No. 12.]

RESOLUTION for the relief of certain parties holding State Witness and Jury Scrip.

Be it resolved by the Senate and House of Representatives of the State of Florida in General Assembly convened, That the Treasurer of the State of Florida be and he is hereby authorized to pay the Jury Certificate No. 63, given to George A. Turknet at the March term, 1856, of the Circuit Court for the county of Duval, State of Florida, amounting to Fifteen Dollars, without endorsement of said Turknet, he being dead; also the State Witness Certificate No. 54, given to John Townsend at the March term of the Circuit Court for Duval county, A. D. 1857, amounting to Two Dollars, without being endorsed, the said John Townsend being dead; also State Witness Certificate No. 2, given to John W. Price at the spring term of Circuit Court of Nassau county, A. D. 1857, amounting to Five Dollars, the Clerk's report for said county not having been sent in to the Comptroller.

Treasurer authorized certain Jury and Witness certificates.

Passed the Senate December 14, 1859. Passed the House of Representatives December 19, 1859. Approved by the Governor December 21, 1859.

[No. 13.]

JOINT RESOLUTION for the relief of Andrew J. Lanier, of Lafayette county.

Be it resolved by the Senate and House of Representa-
Released as security on bond of Green Butler. *tives of the State of Florida in General Assembly convened,* That Andrew J. Lanier, of the county of Lafayette, be and is hereby released from the payment of a certain bond, assigned by him as security for the appearance of one Green Bustle at the fall term of the Circuit Court for Lafayette county, of the Suwannee Circuit, of this State, for 1859.

Passed the Senate December 19, 1859. Passed the House of Representatives December 21, 1859. Approved by the Governor December 22, 1859.

[No. 14.]

RESOLUTION for the relief of J. C. Crosby, late Sheriff of Escambia county.

Be it resolved by the Senate and House of Represonta-
tives of the State of Florida in General Assembly con-
Comptroller to audit claims for apprehending certain criminals *vened,* That the Comptroller of Public Accounts be and he is hereby authorized and required to audit and issue his warrant for the claims of J. C. Crosby, late Sheriff of Escambia county, for services rendered and expenses paid by him in apprehending and committing to jail certain negro thieves
Proviso. in Escambia county: *Provided,* The said J. C. Crosby present to said Comptroller full and satisfactory vouchers and receipts, and full evidence of the facts of said expenses in said claim.

Passed the Senate December 19, 1859. Passed the House of Representatives December 21, 1859. Approved by the Governor December 22, 1859.

[No. 15.]

RESOLUTION for the relief of William Newbern, a Soldier of the War of 1812-'14.

WHEREAS, It appears from certificates and proofs duly adduced, that William Newbern is entitled to relief from the United States Government, as an invalid pensioner, which he has not received; AND WHEREAS, He was a Soldier under one of our greatest chieftains, the immortal Jackson, at the time of his most decided action; AND WHEREAS, In the discharge of his duty as a Soldier for his country, he was severely wounded and has been and still is disabled in consequence of said wound—Therefore,

Preamble.

Be it resolved by the Senate and House of Representatives of the State of Florida in General Assembly convened, That our Senators in Congress be and they are hereby required, and our Representative is requested, to use such measures and take such steps, either before Congress or the Departments at Washington, as may secure due, legal and sufficient compensation to the said William Newbern.

Requesting delegation in Congress to procure compensation for.

Passed the Senate December 17, 1859. Passed the House of Repretentatives December 21, 1859. Approved by the Governor December 22, 1859.

INDEX

TO THE

ACTS AND RESOLUTIONS

OF THE

ADJOURNED SESSION----9th GENERAL ASSEMRLY.

ADDISON, JOHN: Act for relief of, and others,   -   -   73

ADDISON, JOHN S.: Authorized to assume management of estate,   86

APALACHICOLA & NEW ORLEANS STEAM NAVIGATION
COMPANY: Act to incorporate, -   -   -   37

APALACHICOLA & COLUMBUS STEAMBOAT COMPANY: Act
to incorporate,   -   -   -   -   40

APALACHICOLA: Resolution requesting the building of fortifications at,   -   -   -   -   -   99

APPEAL: From Board of County Commissioners, when may be
taken,   -   -   -   -   -   23

Appeal bond, by whom approved,   -   -   -   23

To be tried *de novo*,   -   -   -   -   23

From Courts of Probate, to be tried *de novo* and by jury,   - 26

APPROPRIATIONS: Act making, for fiscal years 1859 and 1860,   . 91

ATSEENA-OTIE: Act to amend act to incorporate city of,   - 54

Powers of City Council of,   -   -   55

ATTACHMENT: Act to amend Attachment Laws,   -   -   16

When writ to issue, oath of party applying for, -   -   16

BAY PORT: Act to create and regulate Pilotage at, -   -   65

BLOCKER, H. T.: Act for relief of,   -   -   -   76

BOARD OF EDUCATION: (See Education.)

BOUNDARY Line between Georgia and Florida established,   - 28

Titles to land derived from Georgia confirmed,   -   -   28

BOWDEN, J. E.: Resolution authorizing pay to, for writing up
Senate Journal,   -   -   -   -   -   101

BREVARD COUNTY: Act for filling offices in,   -   -   62

Sheriff of, to be ex-officio Tax-Assessor and Collector,   -   62

BRONSON, JOHN W.: Authorized to assume management of est.,   84

CALHOUN COUNTY: Offices of Judge of Probate, Clerk and Sh'ff,
    where to be kept, - - - - 67
    Act to be submitted to voters for approval, - - 67
    Judge of Probate to give notice, - - - 67
    Duty of Canvassers, - - - 67

CAMERON, DONALD: Resolution for relief of, - - 100

CHACE, THOMAS J.: Authorized to assume management of estate,   88

CIRCUIT COURT: Time of holding in Hamilton and Taylor counties changed, - - - - 59

CLAY COUNTY: Boundary Lines of—county site—part of annexed to Putnam county, - - - 63

CLERK OF CIRCUIT COURT: When to issue certificates against State for costs to witnesses for defendant in criminal cases, - - - - - 19
    To make reversed index, - - - 26
    Fee therefor, - - - - 27

COLUMBIA COUNTY: Boundary between Columbia and Suwannee counties,) - - - - 69

COMMON SCHOOLS: Superintendent of, to pay amount of school money apportioned, annually to Judges of Probate, - 25
    Judges of Probate to contract for teacher of - 25
    Laws to be published for distribution, - - 95

COMPTROLLER: Duty in reference to payment of certain Volunteer Companies, - - - 24
    Resolution for relief of, - - - 97
    May receive compensation for signing banking bills, - 98

CONE, DAVID N.: Authorized to assume management of estate, 88

CONSTABLE: Fees for summoning jury of inquest and attending - - 18

CORONER: Penalty for failure to execute and return process, including fees therefor, - - - 15

COSTS: Fees to Commissioners, to take testimony, to be taxed in - 18
    In criminal cases, when may be taxed against State, certificates therefor to be issued by Clerk, - 19
    Plaintiff pays when recovery does not exceed fifty dollars, 29

COUNTY COMMISSIONERS: (See Appeal.) mileage of, - 25

COURTS, CIRCUIT: (See Circuit Court.)

COURTS OF PROBATE: Act in relation to, - - 26
    To be considered at all times open, - - 26
    Appeals from, to be tried de novo and by jury, - 26

CROOM, SUSAN M.: Authorized to assume management of estate, 87

CROSBY, J. C.: Resolution for relief of, - - 102

DILWORTH, W. S.: Act for relief of, - - 78

DOUGLASS, ALEXANDER: Act for relief of,   -   -   90
EDUCATION, BOARD OF: Authorized to confer collegiate degrees,   29
EDWARDS, SIMEON A.: Act for relief of,   -   -   -   74
EJECTMENT: Fictitious parties abolished—what declaration in,
    to contain—form of,   -   -   -   -   17
    Plea of not guilty, what to put in issue,   -   -   18
EVERITT, EDMOND N.: Authorized to assume management of
    estate,   -   -   -   -   -   83
EXECUTORS AND ADMINISTRATORS: Returns of, when may
    be made,   -   -   -   -   -   26
    Forfeiture of Commissions for failure to make,   -   -   26
FAIRBANK, HARRISON: Act for relief of,   -   -   -   80
FEES of Constables for summoning jury of inquest and attending
    same,   -   -   -   -   -   18
    Of Commissioners for taking testimony,   -   -   18
    Of Sheriffs for levying execution,   -   -   -   19
FERRY: Across Ocklawaha river,   -   -   -   -   80
    From main land to Way Key,   -   -   -   81
    Across Suwannee river,   -   -   -   82
FIRE-ARMS: Unnecessary use of, on Sunday prohibited,   -   22
FORT: Resolution requesting building of, at Apalachicola,   -   99
FRISBY, GEORGE: Name changed,   -   -   -   89
GADSDEN COUNTY: Boundary Line between Calhon and Lib-
    erty counties,   -   -   -   -   68
    Where suits to be prosecuted,   -   -   -   68
GATES, JOSIAH: Error in act for relief of, and how corrected,   75
GIBSON, ALLEN: Act for relief of,   -   -   -   77
GOODS, WRECKED AND DERELICT: Act for the protection
    and disposal of,   -   -   -   -   20
GOVERNOR: To provide for payment of certain Volunteer Com-
    panies,   -   -   -   -   24
    May fill all vacancies in Brevard county and remove any
        person by him appointed,   -   -   -   62
    Authorized to surrender title of State to land derived from
        Georgia,   -   -   -   -   95
    May unite with Georgia to procure surrender from U. S.,   -   96
    May direct nolle prosequics to be entered, when,   -   -   96
    Authorized to sell bonds to pay loan, for which they are
        pledged,   -   -   -   -   97
GREEN, WILLIAM F.: Authorized to assume management of est.,   84
GUARDIANS: Returns of, when may be made   -   -   26
    For taking of Commissions for miners to make,   -   -   23
GULF CITY & INTERIOR RAILROAD COMPANY: Act in re-
    lation to, act to incorporate,   -   -   -   30
HALLIDAY, SOLOMON F.: Act for relief of,   -   -   77

HAMILTON COUNTY: Time of holding Circuit Court in, changed,   59
HENDRY, JAMES E.; Act for the benefit of heirs of,   -   -   70
HILL, JOHN M.: Act for relief of,   -   -   -   72
HILLSBOROUGH COUNTY: Act to provide for recording marks
    and brands of cattle shipped from,   -   -   60
        Appointment of inspector and duties of,   -   -   60
HOUCK, DAVID F.: Authorized to assume management of estate,   86
HUGHEY, THOMAS: Resolution allowing claims of, for transpor-
    tation of troops,   -   -   -   -   100
INDICTMENT: Against Sheriff for failure to execute and return
    process,   -   -   -   -   -   15
        Against person finding wrecked or derelict goods who shall
            fail to report same to Judge of Probate,   -   -   21
        Against Commissioners and overseers of roads for neglect of
            duty,   -   -   -   -   -   27
        Against masters of vessels for violating quarantine regulations
            of City Council of City of Atseena Otie,   -   -   55
        For injury or obstruction to St. Johns and Indian river Canal,   58
INTERNAL IMPROVEMENT: Part of 24th section of Internal
    Improvement act forbidding certain branches of roads
    to North boundary line, repealed,   -   -   27
JUDGE OF PROBATE: Duty and compensation of, in reference
    to wrecked or derelict goods,   -   -   -   21
        To contract for teacher of Common Schools,   -   -   25
        To appropriate Common School money,   -   -   25
JURY SCRIP: Treasurer authorized to pay certain jury scrip,   -   101
JUSTICES OF THE PEACE: May fine for failure to report
    wrecked or derelict goods,   -   -   -   21
        May fine for unnecessary use of fire arms on Sunday,   -   22
KING, MARY: Name changed to Mary Hancock,   -   -   90
LAKE CITY & SUWANNEE RAILROAD COMPANY: Act to
    incorporate,   -   -   -   -   -   44
LAKE CITY: Act to correct an error in printed act to incorporate
    City of,   -   -   -   -   -   53
LAND: Titles to, derived from Georgia confirmed,   -   -   28
LANIER, ANDREW J.: Resolution for relief of,   -   -   102
LIBERTY COUNTY: Boundary Line between Liberty and Gads-
    den counties,   -   -   -   -   -   68
        Where suits to be prosecuted,   -   -   -   68
LICENSE: To retail spiritous liquors, when may be issued and
    how taken out,   -   -   -   -   20
MAIL ROUTE: Resolution asking change of,   -   -   99
MANATEE COUNTY: (See Marks and Brands.)
        Road laws of Duval county made applicable to,   -   -   62
MANNING, LITTLEBERRY: Authorized to assume management

of estate,   -   -   -   -   -   85
MARKS AND BRANDS: Act to provide for recording of, of cattle
   shipped from Manatee and Hillsborough counties,   -   60
   Appointment and duties of Inspector of,   -   -   60
MARTIN, G. W.: Authorized to establish ferry,   -   -   82
McCASKIL, KENNETH: Act for relief of,   -   -   -   90
MILITIA: Act to amend Militia and Patrol laws,   -   -   9
MOORE, A. J.: Act for relief of,   -   -   -   -   78
NEWBERN, WILLIAM: Resolution for relief of,   -   -   102
NEW RIVER COUNTY: Error as to interest on railroad bonds
   corrected, ...   69
NEWSOMS, HUGH M.: Name changed to Hugh M. Keen,   .   89
NOTARY PUBLIC: Act regulating fees of, in St. Johns county,   .   67
OCKLAWAHA RIVER: Trustees of Internal Imp. authorized to
   contract to clear out, ...   29
ORANGE COUNTY: Division of moneys between Orange and Vo-
   lusia counties, ...   61
   Proceedings against Treasurer for failure to pay,   .   .   61
PAPY, M. F.: Act for relief of, ...   77
PATROL: Act to amend Militia and Patrol laws,   .   .   9
PEARCE, WILLIAM: Act for relief of adm'r of estate of,   -   80
PEARSON, JOHN W.: Authorized to establish ferry,   -   -   80
PENSACOLA: Act more fully defining duties of Tax Assessor and
   Collector of,   -   -   -   -   -   49
   Proceedings when taxes are unpaid,   -   -   -   49–50
   Sale of property and redemption by owner,   -   -   50
   Bidding, how to be made,   -   -   -   -   50
   Taxes on land held in common or parcenary to be charged on
   the whole,   -   -   -   -   -   51
   Mayor of, authorized to determine violations of ordinances,
   and impose and enforce punishments,   -   -   51
   Who eligible as Appraiser or Tax Assessor,   -   -   51
   Bond and oath of Tax Assessor of,   -   -   -   51
   City of, authorized to endorse or guarantee bonds of Alabama
   and Florida Railroad Company—limitation,   -   54
   Mayor and Aldermen of, authorized to elect and remove
   Weigher of Cotton—when,   -   -   -   55
   Mayor may fill vacancy,   -   -   -   -   56
   Act amending Pilot laws for,   -   -   -   66
   Combination between allowed,   -   -   -   66
   What vessels liable and what exempt,   -   -   66
   Pilots to be furnished with copy of laws,   -   -   66
PENSACOLA AND GEORGIA RAILROAD COMPANY: Act in
   relation to—act to incorporate amended,   -   -   30

PERDIDO RAIL ROAD COMPANY—Grant of alternate sections
    land to,   -   -   -   -   -   50
PERDIDO RIVER: Declared navigable,   -   -   -   44
PHYSICIANS AND SURGEONS: May file certified copies of Di-
    ploma with Clerk Circuit Court,   -   -   -   22
    Exempt from road duty,   -   -   -   27–8
PILOTAGE: Act to regulate at Bay Port,   -   -   -   65
    Act amending pilot laws for Pensacola,   -   -   66
PRICE, SPENCER: Authorized to establish ferry,   -   -   81
PRICE, JOHN W.: Treasurer to pay witness certificate issued to,   101
PUTNAM COUNTY: Part of Clay County annexed to, -   -   63
QUARANTINE: Penalty on Masters of vessels violating regula-
    tions established by City Council of City of Atseena Otie,   54
QUINCY: Act to amend act entitled act to incorporate town of,   52
RECORDS: Clerk of Circuit Court to make reversed index,   -   26
REGISTER, U. S.: Authorized to occupy room in Capitol free of
    charge,   -   -   -   -   -   98
RESOLUTION: Instructing Delegates in Congress to prefer charges
    against certain members thereof, -   -   -   96–7
    Asking change of mail route,   -   -   90
    Requesting building of Fort at Apalachicola,   -   -   99
REVELL, ANDREW J.: name changed to Andrew J. Duncan,   -   90
ROADS: Acts concerning,   -   -   -   -   27
    Indictment against Commissioners and Overseers of, for ne-
    glect of duty, ...   27
SHEPARD, H. M.: Act for relief of guardian of heirs of,   .   78
SHEPARD, ISAAC N.: Act for relief of,   .   .   .   79
SHERIFFS: Act concerning—penalty for failing to execute and
    return process—indictment for—penalty for to whom
    paid, ...   15
    Penalty for false return—action therefor—act extended to
    criminal cases—security of Sheriff, for what liable,   .   16
    Levying execution, entitled to commissions,   .   19
    Duty of in reference to wrecked or derelict goods,   .   21
SMITH, JOSEPH D.: Authorized to assume management of estate,   83
SMITH, GEORGE GIBBS: Name changed,   .   .   .   89
SPIRITOUS LIQUOR: License to retail, when may be issued,
    and how taken out, ...   20
    Quantities of one quart and upwards may be drank where
    bought, ...   23
ST. JOHNS COUNTY: Act regulating fees of Notary Public in,   .   69
ST. JOHNS AND INDIAN RIVER CANAL: Act to secure right
    of way to, ...   50
    Grant of right of way over State land lands—right to enter

upon lands of individuals—use timber, &c.—compensation therefor—proceedings to assess value of, . . . 57

Forfeiture for injury or obstruction to, . . . 58

SUGGS, NOAH P.: Act for relief of, . . . 71

SUNDAY: Unnecessary use of fire-arms on, prohibited, . 22

Penalty for, ... 22

SUWANNEE COUNTY: Error as to interest on Railroad bonds corrected, ... 69

Boundary between Suwannee and Columbia counties, . 69

TAXATION: Act to amend act to establish ad valorem system, amended, ... 20

TAXES: Time for collecting, extended, . . . 19

Of City of Pensacola, how collected, . . . 50

Sale of property and redemption by owner, . . 50

Biddings, how to be made, ... 50

On land held in common or parcenary, charged on the whole, 51

TAX ASSESSOR & COLLECTOR: Of Pensacola, act more fully defining duties of, ... 49

Proceedings of, when taxes remain unpaid, . . 49–50

Oath and bond of, ... 57

TAX COLLECTOR: When to make returns to Comptroller, . 19

TAYLOR COUNTY: Time of holding Circuit Court in, changed, . 59

TOWNSEND, JOHN: Treasurer authorized to pay witness certificate issued to, ... 101

TRUSTEES OF INT. IMP. FUND: Authorized to contract to clear out Ocklawaha river, ... 29

May pledge land or value thereof in money therefor, . 29–30

Authorized to grant alternate sections to Perdido Railroad Company, ... 59

TUCKER, WILLIAM W.: Authorized to assume management of estate, ... 82

TURKNET, G. A.: Treasurer to pay jury scrip issued to, . 101

VACANCIES: In Brevard county, Governor may fill, . . 62

VOLUNTEERS: Act for payment of, for services previous to being mustered in, ... 24

Due proof of service to be made to Comptroller, . . 24

VOLUSIA COUNTY: Act to amend act to organize county of . 61

Division of monies between Orange and Volusia counties, . 61

Proceedings against Treasurer for failure to pay, . 61

Act to unite offices of Judge of Probate and Clerk of Circuit Court, ... 70

WALKER, MINOR W.: Authorized to assume management of est., 87

WALTON COUNTY: County Commissioners of, may receive and loan out Common School Fund, . . . 63

County Commissioners authorized to levy a bridge tax, how
   appropriated, ...   64–5
WASHINGTON COUNTY: Where Clerk's office to be kept,   .   64
WEIGHER: Of Cotton in Pensacola, who may elect and remove,   55
   Vacancy, how filled, ...   56
   Oath, duties and liability of and allowances to, .   .   56
WEST, CHARLES M.: Authorized to assume management of est.,   85
WILKINS, PETER C.: Act for relief of,   .   .   90
WILLIFORD, SAMUEL B.: Act for relief of,   .   .   75
WITNESS CERTIFICATES: Treasurer authorized to pay certain
   certificates, ...   101
WRECKED AND DERELICT GOODS: Act for the protection
   and disposal of, ...   20

www.ingramcontent.com/pod-product-compliance
Lightning Source LLC
Chambersburg PA
CBHW030538270326
41927CB00008B/1430